The Funeral Celebrant's Handbook

The Funeral Celebrant's Handbook

Creating services that celebrate life and mourn death

Barry H. Young

JoJo

PUBLISHING

The right of Barry Young to be identified as the author of this work has been asserted
by him in accordance with the Copyright Designs and Patent Act 1988.

© Barry Young 2008

National Library of Australia Cataloguing-in-Publication data:

The funeral celebrant's handbook.

By Barry H Young.

Published by JoJo Publishing

'Yarra's Edge'
2203/80 Lorimer Street
Docklands VIC 3008
Australia

Email: jo-media@bigpond.net.au or visit www.jojopublishing.com

© 2008 JoJo Publishing

National Library of Australia
Cataloguing-in-Publication data
      Young, Barry H
      The funeral celebrant's handbook

      ISBN 9780980321616 (hbk.)
      ISBN 9780987410320 (pbk.)

Subjects: Funeral rites and ceremonies--Handbooks, manuals, etc.

      393.9

Editor: Emma Driver
Designer / typesetter: Rob Ryan @ Z Design Media
Printed in China by Everbest Printing

Love doesn't end with dying,
Or leave with the last breath.

For someone you have loved dearly,
Love goes on forever.

— Anon

Contents

Part 3 Sample Services

Part 4 Some Inspiration

Preface

It is now widely accepted that the need for religious ceremonies at both weddings and funerals is a thing of the past. Today the number of weddings conducted by a qualified civil celebrant have reached a staggering high in Australia. Likewise, the demand for funeral services prepared by a funeral celebrant, in collaboration with family members and friends of the deceased, is ever increasing.

There is a deep human need to encompass and surround important events in life with rituals, symbolism and expressions of beliefs. Both religious and non-religious people have the same right to, and need for, meaningful cultural rituals and celebration. However, with an increasing number of people not practising religious ceremonies on a regular basis, there is a need for funerals that are not bound by the doctrines of any specific religious creed. The need has arisen for funeral celebrants to step into the void, and to develop and present services in harmony with the deceased's own beliefs.

Life-centred funerals

Today's need is for an individually prepared ceremony with appropriate wording based on the life of the person who has died, with emphasis on celebrating the life rather than focusing on death. A life-centred or personal funeral is one that primarily recognises and pays tribute to the departed, and records and remembers the life that has been lived. It allows mourners to let go of their emotions, to experience them and to face the reality of death.

Most mourners do not come to a funeral to hear a sermon about sin or to philosophise about death. They come to grieve, to share with others, and to reflect on the life of their lost one and what is meaningful in life. They come to be comforted and uplifted in their time of need.

The advantage that a funeral celebrant's service has over a traditional religious service is that it is not restricted by the old rituals of the church, which are not always in harmony with the beliefs of the bereaved and the deceased. People are now free to experiment with a wide range of beliefs, and to express a wide range of meaningful rituals as part of a tailored service.

Planning tailored services

A non-religious or personal service must be planned with great attention to detail, and delivered with care and sensitivity. Naturally, if the advantage of the funeral celebrant is to be able to tailor each service to what is meaningful for the bereaved, then each service must be planned from scratch with a great deal of care.

The true advantage of using funeral celebrants to conduct a funeral is that celebrants can plan the service to the family's requirements. The family of the deceased should have the service they want and not have any rituals imposed upon them. This freedom of choice gives those who are grieving a chance to be part of the process of organising the funeral service for their loved one.

A person's life deserves the finest of celebrations and ceremonies possible, both through the written word and the presentation of the service. It is therefore the celebrant's role to select the best of literature, ritual, music and symbolism. It may also be our role to write a creative eulogy to reflect on the life and achievements of the deceased if requested by the family. Thus, the service should help the bereaved to live through their feelings, recognise the meaning and reality of death, and hopefully help those grieving people to accept the loss of their loved one and to resume their lives without the presence of that person.

As a celebrant you should not be afraid to make suggestions. Good funeral celebrants should discuss every possibility when they talk over their service details. After meeting with the family and friends of the deceased, the celebrant will be able to develop an empathy with the deceased and, if the meeting has been properly conducted, this will allow the funeral celebrant to conduct a meaningful and memorable service.

Assisting the grieving process

The pain of grief is great, and it is the celebrant's duty to prepare a service that is accurate, authentic and appropriate, turning a distressing event into a beautiful, meaningful memory.

The grieving process is a painful and complex event in the lives of the bereaved— and the funeral service is the single most important part of expressing grief. It is also the first stage of the healing process, as it allows the bereaved the opportunity to express their grief. Thus, it is the duty of the celebrant to conduct a reverent and dignified salute to the deceased and a comforting and meaningful event for the survivors.

Spiritual services

I strongly believe that even a non-religious service has spiritual elements. Some of my readings, personally written, have a spiritual meaning, and in choosing a civil service rather than a religious service the bereaved need not ignore higher meaning and religious beliefs. Not surprisingly, prayers and readings with a spiritual element are often requested by mourners.

Sharing my experience

The aim of this book is to help existing celebrants who are licensed to officiate at funerals and those who are aspiring to become funeral celebrants. I have endeavoured to set out—in basic language—the format of a funeral service and the practical measures that need to be taken. Those who are new to this topic will find many aspects of a funeral service they won't have even imagined, and that are not mentioned in the academic courses that celebrants are now required to complete to become qualified. While written in the context of Australian funeral procedure, the information in this book can be adapted to any country in the world.

This book is written from the heart and is based on the down-to-earth, hard-won experience that I hope to share with you. When I began there was no such thing as a course for funeral celebrants. My only resource was Dally Messenger, the pioneer and the master. His book, *Ceremonies for Today*, was more relevant for marriage celebrants than funeral celebrants, but we all used it—and still do. The vision and scholarship of Dally Messenger has made my career and this book possible.

Those of my era learnt the hard way and, with all due respect to the courses now in existence, you won't find many of the important things I share with you in their curricula. This is what makes this handbook so important for our difficult, unsung profession.

Writing from my experience of conducting funerals for all types of people—the elderly, the middle-aged, children, babies, tragic accidents, suicides and murders—I will tell it as I think it should be told, and help you write and conduct a responsible, caring and meaningful service.

This handbook covers every aspect of a service, beginning at the time of initial contact with family or friends of the deceased and the first meeting with the bereaved , up to the conclusion of the funeral service.

There are no firm rules on how to conduct a service. Every service is different and should be tailored tastefully to meet the wishes of the family or friends and the personality of the person who has passed. However, while we are obliged to tailor each service we are not left to start from scratch every time. With experience you soon develop a collection of readings, rituals, verses, sayings and songs that you can

interweave with ideas expressed by the bereaved to create a new and unique service for each life you are asked to celebrate.

The highest rewards

Whether it is a funeral service to celebrate a human life that has ended, in the case of the elderly, or to officiate at a tragic event, the purpose is the same—to provide mutual support and comfort to the living. It's a task that I never take lightly and one that should be considered a great honour.

The greatest reward that I can ever be given is when mourners have asked me after a service whether I was a personal friend of the deceased. Others have complimented me on getting the tone of the service 'just right'. It's then you know you have really made an important contribution to a very significant and spiritual day in many people's lives.

The task that a celebrant must undertake is to juggle the multiple roles of interviewer, listener, biographer, creative writer, psychologist and entertainer. It's a difficult job but an important and rewarding one.

It has been a privilege to be a part of the sacred, spiritual rituals of so many families and friends who have said goodbye to loved ones at my services over the years. It's also a great honour to be able to share my many years of experience with you in this handbook.

I hope that you will find the ideas and explanations in these pages to be a valuable guiding hand as you create your own services for your own communities, and I will be thrilled to think that I have played some small role in spreading the practice of quality, tailored funeral celebrations.

May you find your path as rewarding as I have found mine in bringing comfort and strength to those in their time of need.

Barry H. Young

About the author

Barry H. Young is better known as an author of historical literature. He has forged a reputation as Australia's most prominent author of American Western Frontier novels. *River of Dreams*, *Reign of Terror*, *Shadows on the Lonesome Trail* and *Triumph of Hate* are some of his best-known works. His writings have been described as 'pure poetry'.

Barry retired from a successful career as the director of sales and marketing with the Gas and Fuel Corporation of Victoria and, after moving to New South Wales, was engaged by John Hossack Funeral Services in Albury to conduct non-religious funeral services.

He has carried out this work for many years and now looks upon the conducting of funeral services as a calling. He is always mindful of a family's grief and brings them comfort and new found strength. The personal satisfaction he has received in this calling has compelled him to share his knowledge and experiences with aspiring funeral celebrants.

Barry has been a member of the Australian Federation of Civil Celebrants since 1998. He From his many years as a funeral celebrant, he has put together a vast range of information that makes this book a compulsory study for all existing and aspiring funeral celebrants. His uniquely structured funeral services and his creative writing experience has put new meaning into this solemn and heart-wrenching occasion.

Barry was awarded an Order of Australia on Australia Day in 2008 for meritorious service to the community through support for a range of youth, service and aged care organisations and grief counselling.

He lives with his wife, Bev, and family in the beautiful Thurgoona Valley in New South Wales.

PART
1

About the Funeral Service

1 *What you should know about funerals*

The information in this chapter is a collection of general tips for celebrants. We will look at different aspects of funeral services—your role as the celebrant, types of funeral, and some challenging situations you might face. Then, in the chapters that follow, we'll discuss in more detail each part of the preparation and performance of the funeral service.

What are the celebrant's responsibilities?

As a funeral celebrant, or as someone studying to become a celebrant, the first thing you should be clear about is your own role in the funeral service.

The celebrant's key responsibility is to meet with the family of the deceased and methodically record details of the life of the deceased, so that what is written depicts the true character of that person. With the bereaved family and/or friends, you will put together an outline of the service. A personal service, properly prepared, can then be delivered with confidence, care and sensitivity. The aim of this is to help and support family and other mourners who are struggling with the reality of their loved one's death.

The funeral director's role is to arrange the service, then support the celebrant during the delivery of the service. If it is a chapel service, the celebrant will rely on the expert timing of the funeral director to support announcements of music, PowerPoint presentations, videos or DVDs. Funeral directors are also responsible for other matters such as handing out orders of service, ushering, seating, flower arrangements on the coffin, placement of memorabilia and photos, and so on. If it is a graveside service, then it is the role of the funeral director to make all preparations for the service in conjunction with the cemetery. The role of the celebrant then is to deliver the service.

The importance of team effort

It has been my privilege to have conducted funerals services in conjunction with excellent funeral directors, and I cannot stress enough the importance of a team effort. You, as the celebrant, and the funeral director need to work closely together to create a professional, meaningful ceremony for the bereaved. To do this, you need to see yourself as a team member, and communicate with the funeral director throughout your preparation to make sure nothing is missed. Work with the funeral director and staff to make their tasks easier and they will do the same to help with yours.

When planning the ceremony with the bereaved, I always reassure them that the funeral director they have chosen is very professional, and that they are in excellent and caring hands.

Types of ceremonies and services

I believe the word *ceremony* can be rightfully used to celebrate the life of a person who has lived a long, full and purposeful life. When the elderly depart we recognise a natural change, something which is normal—a lifetime and life span lived to encompass all that was to be given and achieved.

But the passing of a young person shocks us as it seems so unfair, so needless a waste of a life that had so much to give—mountains to climb, rivers to cross, challenges to be faced and conquered. Accordingly, I refer to these occasions as *services*.

Thus, a ceremony or service that meets the needs of those who grieve for an elderly person who died peacefully will not be the same as the service for those who have lost a child.

How long should a service be?

Invariably, families say to me, 'We want a brief and simple service'. You will hear this on many occasions. But how brief is 'brief'? How simple is 'simple'?

A family's instructions must be respected, but if there is a story to be told about the deceased then it should be told. And everyone's idea of 'brief' is different so it's hard to know how far you need to go. No celebrant worth their salt should conduct a service that is effectively a 'Hail and farewell' or 'Hello and goodbye'. This is not only abrupt, but disrespectful to the deceased.

Without exception I have found that families requesting a brief service have little idea what a brief service is. Every time I have reluctantly contained the service to comply with the family's request for brevity, the family has afterwards expressed a wish that I had spoken for longer.

Generally, I endeavour to plan a memorable service that will run for at least 20 minutes, and hopefully much more. The length of the service, of course, depends on the number of speakers, the music and other acceptable inclusions, such as bereaved friends and family placing flowers or touching the coffin.

I always write a complete eulogy, even when a family member or friend will be the main speaker. After the speaker or speakers have finished, I then sum up, ensuring all the information is covered. This also means that if any speakers falter, the day is not lost.

All these factors affect the length of the service and make it special and meaningful for the bereaved, so you should never place a time limit on a service.

A graveside service

Where a graveside service is to be conducted, I generally take up a position with the funeral director and lead pallbearers carrying the coffin or casket* from the hearse to the grave. Being a pallbearer has special meaning for them as they are able to render a last act of love and respect. If pallbearers are taking part in the service, the funeral director will direct them in their duties.

Hopefully, some sort of marquee or gazebo will be available should the weather turn inclement. Most council-operated cemeteries have portable undercover marquees or gazebos available which they will erect on request. Do think ahead and have a plan should the weather turn against you—the service will be greatly affected if you are left to stand in a hailstorm.

At an open-air graveside service you should always have umbrellas on hand for both mourners and yourself, whether the sun is shining brightly or rain is tumbling down. Should the heavens open, ask a member of the funeral director's staff to hold an umbrella over you to safeguard your notes.

I once conducted a service where the rain was so heavy that the sound of it falling on the umbrellas drowned out my words to all except those close by. You can't always be unaffected by every contingency, but you can certainly plan for as many as possible.

Setting up the graveside area

Always make sure the funeral director has a lectern for your to rest your notes on. If one is not available, you can make do with whatever has been used for the guestbook—simply wait until the mourners are assembled and you can reuse this device.

Seating for immediate family and the elderly should be in place. Elderly or frail mourners should not be asked to stand for any length of time.

Make sure that an amplification system is available, particularly if the gathering will be large. I once conducted a service to 300 mourners and had to shout the whole way through as the funeral director forgot the audio equipment. Needless to say, shouting is not appropriate.

---

* Some funeral directors insist on using the word 'coffin' while others like to refer to the same item as a 'casket'. Both are acceptable. Many funeral directors who use the term 'casket' do so because they believe it to be a more gentle word than 'coffin'.

If music is requested, check with the funeral director that the appropriate player will be on hand. Always ask the funeral director to arrange for a staff member to operate the sound system and music as required, so you can concentrate on other tasks.

If the weather is uncomfortable due to heat, the funeral director should have a supply of chilled water available to offer to distressed mourners.

Lowering the coffin or casket

This is a very poignant part of the service. Most funeral directors lower the casket to its full extent but I believe the casket should be lowered only partly into the grave. This prevents the process taking too long—being the final act, the mourners' grief will be unnecessarily prolonged if it seems to go on and on. Of course, the casket can be lowered to the full depth of the grave at a later stage when mourners have departed.

In a subtle way, you might also be able to remind the funeral director to make sure the lowering device works. I have conducted services during which the coffin could not be lowered due to a faulty mechanism. Everything should be checked to avoid such issues, as you only get one chance to get things right.

Scattering dust or ashes

Traditionally a container of sand is made available for scattering over the coffin as it is lowered. This may be important to some and certainly has a traditional religious history, but I have never been a great supporter of this procedure.

Ashes are not so prevalent as in the past but if they are requested then you may work in conjunction with the funeral director to provide them. It is their responsibility to obtain the ashes and yours to then conduct the service.

Flowers

The once-popular wreath adorning the coffin has now been replaced by an arrangement of flowers, often with colours requested by the family. Such a creation is not compulsory but in a decorative sense can add warmth and expression to a solemn occasion. Most funeral parlours work in conjunction with an established florist.

Some families and friends of the deceased will bring flowers cut from their gardens and, at the invitation of the celebrant, come forward and place them on the coffin.

Memorabilia

It sometimes provides comfort to mourners to place certain articles of particular significance on the coffin after it is lowered into the grave. I have witnessed a football, cricket bat, baseball glove, a complete set of golf clubs, bottles of whisky, a deck of cards, a Mars Bar, team jumpers, scarves and more being placed on coffins.

My favourite item was a saw. The deceased had been a carpenter, and the saw was left with him 'just in case he wanted to get out'.

A chapel service followed by a graveside burial

At a burial or committal held at a cemetery after the main ceremony at the chapel, the celebrant should speak for no longer than about five to eight minutes. The main part of the service, including tributes, readings and the eulogy, have already occurred, and there is no point in prolonging the grief of the mourners.

When a chapel service is followed by a graveside burial the celebrant's role is as follows.

- When the service is completed in the chapel, the funeral director will ask the pallbearers to come forward and take their places alongside the coffin.

- The celebrant then leads the cortege from the chapel to the waiting hearse.

- When the hearse arrives at the cemetery, the celebrant leads the cortege from the hearse to grave, together with the funeral director.

A memorial service

A memorial service is a service where the body is not present. It is an occasion that allows everyone to say goodbye. It is important to acknowledge the life of the deceased and to help the family and friends accept that their loved one is no longer with them. All present have the opportunity to say goodbye with love, peace and dignity.

Reasons for a memorial service vary. There may be extenuating circumstances. The deceased may have passed overseas—a victim of war, for example. Perhaps the deceased has willed that their body be donated to science. A body may be not released by a coroner if the circumstances of the death are under investigation. When a very private cremation or burial service has been held with only close family, a memorial service then allows friends of the deceased to say farewell.

I have conducted several memorial services at the home of the deceased or family members after a private burial service was held elsewhere. Once I conducted a cremation funeral service in Melbourne, and the next day travelled to Mount Beauty, 250 kilometres away, to conduct a memorial service where the deceased lived for the major part of his life.

I have found that memorial services are not so heart-wrenching for families.

Mourners can be in a state of greater peace and repose, and feel a real part of the service. The fact that the physical presence of the coffin is absent sometimes also helps set the mood of the service. There can be greater flexibility. The emphasis is automatically transferred from the body to the life of the person.

A service without the body

When a death occurs under normal circumstances, the body is usually laid to rest within a short time, but when the bodies cannot be found, a service without a body can be conducted. This situation can arise in times of war, tragic happenings and freak circumstances.

For example, I was once called upon to conduct a service for a young married couple who lost their lives in a light plane accident. At the time of the service the bodies had not been recovered and the family was left with fading hopes—but the outcome was obvious. All knew it was going to be difficult to accept the couple's tragic death without finding the bodies. It was a cruel blow to a wonderful young couple and my concern was how the family and friends would accept the inevitable and carry on with their lives.

It was at this time that I had to convince everyone to dig deep and move on with the grieving process. This was extremely difficult. As we all know, it is not uncommon during the initial stages of grief to feel numb and paralysed. Little gets done and making key decisions becomes nearly impossible.

The service was held without the bodies, much like a memorial service but with a difference. People were invited to speak to recount and reflect on experiences they had shared with the couple, from the light-hearted memories to the more serious remembrances. There were plenty of tears amid much laughter. It was an opportunity for family and friends to get on with grieving, offering a sense of closure for some, and a moment many will cherish all their life.

I urged the family and friends to celebrate the lives that had been lost, challenging them to focus on what they had gained from knowing the deceased, rather than what they had lost. They had both lived full and happy lives, and all those who knew them knew the couple would have wanted their loved ones to do the same. Their legacy will live on.

An elaborate or unusual service

Is there such a thing as a service too elaborate? The answer is 'no'. If elaborate is what the family wants, your role should be to comply with their wishes as best you can. However, it is paramount that you confer with the funeral director and convey any wishes that may not have been discussed at the time of conducting funeral arrangements; obviously costs are involved in certain elaborate arrangements.

Some funerals I have conducted could be termed 'different'. They included features such as:

- incense wafting throughout the chapel

- a service conducted by candlelight

- special lighting requests

- heavy metal music

- motorcycles in the foyer of a chapel

- irregular positioning of the coffin

- the inclusion of pets, once including a cockatoo, which kept screeching a rather rude word

- opera singers present for their fellow deceased performer, which became a concert more than a funeral service

- a performance by a full jazz band.

I considered all but the cockatoo perfectly acceptable.

One meaningful service included a request by the family to light a single candle at the beginning of the service. The candle depicted life, and it flickered throughout the service. After the committal I extinguished the candle, signalling the farewell of the deceased, and then presented it to the family as a token of new life.

A service in conjunction with a clergy member

There is—and probably always will be—a difference of opinion between members of religious clergy and civil celebrants on the matter of who is best qualified to conduct a funeral service. Celebrants have made a significant impact in weddings and funeral services which were once the sole domain of the church. As a funeral celebrant, however, you are not in any way challenging the church, but supplementing it—

you are providing something extra, rather than trying to replace the church.

Occasionally, a family may request that you work alongside a member of the clergy. This may be due to a preference thc deceased made known before their death, or the wishes of a family member. My experience in these situations has varied. In some cases it has been a rewarding and enriching experience; in others I have found my input undervalued or even rejected.

No matter what the situation, however, it is paramount that each party show respect and conduct their duties in a unified manner. The purpose of the funeral service is to recognise and pay tribute to the life of the deceased, and this must remain at the forefront of your mind at all times. Of course it goes without saying that you should maintain your professionalism, even if your presence is opposed. Be courteous and remain respectful of any religious elements the bereaved have requested in the service.

A service in a country cemetery

I have had the privilege to conduct many burial services at some beautiful rural cemeteries in country New South Wales and Victoria. In many cases, one has to adapt to the conditions. Inclement weather can be a problem in smaller rural cemeteries, which may not have the equipment for dealing with extreme heat or rain.

I have found in the majority of cases that when bad weather occurs the cemetery managers have erected shelter in the form of a gazebo or a tent, but this may be something you need to check with the funeral directors or cemetery manager.

If the weather is hot, the funeral director should arrange for an esky of chilled water to be on hand, and for portable seats for the elderly and infirm amongst the bereaved.

An interstate service

There will be occasions that you will be required to travel with the hearse and the funeral director or staff to interstate locations. It is important that you become a team member and share duties on these journeys, offering assistance where possible.

Other elements of funeral services

Viewing the deceased

Whether or not to have a viewing of the deceased is a personal matter for the bereaved to decide. It is an invitation and not a must. Some people find it distasteful, while others receive comfort and look upon the occasion as a time to say goodbye.

The practice to view is gaining favour as modern methods of preparing the deceased have improved remarkably, and leave the deceased looking peaceful and restful. Many funeral directors now actively encourage a viewing.

For those families that choose it, 'the viewing' is an important part of the mourning process. It allows those who wish to say their personal goodbyes, express their love or complete 'unfinished business' to do so. It can help mourners to come to terms with the reality and finality of death; they can see that the one who has passed is now at peace, especially if they had been suffering an illness.

Early on, I was always reluctant to view the deceased at the funeral parlour, but have now overcome that concern. It took me some time to do this but I am now comfortable with it, as I know the preparations are very professional.

Guard of honour

A guard of honour is a popular means of expressing a tribute to the deceased who had a significant affiliation with the representative organisation. Some can be quite spectacular and add a touch of theatre to the service.

Examples include motorcycles, fire engines, rally cars, ambulances, mountain horses, model aeroplanes, sporting teams in full dress, armed forces in full uniform, dogs, and even fishing rods held appropriately.

Music

Most funeral services will have music requested or supplied by the family and friends of the person who has passed.

Your role as the celebrant is to prepare an introduction to each piece of music, and work with the staff member in charge of the audio equipment to make sure the music is ready at the appropriate time—a prearranged signal is a good idea. Don't try to look after the audio equipment yourself.

The introduction can go something like, 'As a tribute to Bert, we will now play one of his favourite songs …' This provides funeral staff the time to cue the music.

Often when a song is playing, the bereaved may become emotional. Wait a while and then just walk over and offer comfort—it's just a little gesture but well appreciated.

Commonly requested songs

- 'Wind Beneath My Wings' (Bette Midler)
- 'Time to Say Goodbye' (Andrea Bocelli and Sarah Brightman)
- 'Amazing Grace' (Harry Secombe)
- 'My Way' (Frank Sinatra)
- 'Nessun Dorma' (The Three Tenors or Luciano Pavarotti)
- 'I'll Walk with God' (Mario Lanza)
- 'You Raise Me Up' (Russell Watson or Josh Groban)
- 'Morning Has Broken' (Cat Stevens)
- 'Softly as I Leave You' (Matt Monro or Elvis Presley)
- 'Climb Every Mountain' (Mormon Tabernacle Choir)
- 'You'll Never Walk Alone' (Mormon Tabernacle Choir)
- 'The Power of Love' (Celine Dion)
- 'The Lord is my Shepherd' (23rd Psalm)
- 'The Lord's Prayer'
- 'Abide with Me'
- 'Angel'

Other requested performers include Bing Crosby, Enya, Vera Lynn, Slim Dusty and Glenn Miller's Big Band.

Organ

Nothing sounds better at a funeral service than the warmth of an organ played well. Usually the organ is used when hymns are to be sung.

I have been very fortunate to have two accomplished musicians that are engaged when the family requests music by an organist. It is useful to seek out these kind of contacts who you might use, or recommend, on such occasions. Funeral parlours will usually be able to help, too.

Committal music

There are varying points of view in respect to playing music as the coffin disappears from view. One view is that it detracts from the intensity of emotion; another is that appropriate music takes away some of the harshness of the moment and makes it more bearable. This is a matter of taste and one for the bereaved to decide.

Unusual musical tastes

Don't be surprised by anything you are asked to play—I have had everything you can imagine requested, from jazz to heavy metal and everything in between.

For example, I was once asked for 'The Chicken Dance' by the family of a German polka fan. People stood to do the dance, too, hopping from one foot to the other and flapping their arms like wings to the music.

On another occasion, the song of the Collingwood AFL club song was requested. The staff member looking after the audio played the Essendon club song by mistake— fortunately it caused a big laugh.

Photos

At time of interview, I always ask the bereaved if they have a photo that can be placed on the coffin or on a table at the front of the chapel. Invariably that suggestion will be taken up, and an appropriate photo located. If a suitable photo is found that needs enlarging or framing, then suggest this be done.

Your request for a photo may result in the family bringing out photo albums and looking through them painstakingly, explaining the events of the photos to you. Always be patient, and gently endeavour to bring back the interview to the structure of the service.

If the family wish to show more than one photo, suggest that a member of the family set up a photo board. This can be done prior to the service.

Videos

The practice of videoing funeral services has become popular. Although it can be somewhat distracting to the celebrant and speakers, it affords the family and friends a memory of this special occasion.

Audiovisual presentations by a family member or friend, depicting events in the deceased's life, are also becoming a more common part of a service. A popular practice is a slide show presentation using PowerPoint or similar software, where photos are displayed in quick rotation on screen. This innovation is particularly poignant when accompanied by the deceased's favourite music or appropriate background music. Usually these are presented by a person who can use the audiovisual equipment and thus does not involve the celebrant. As always, however, the celebrant should prepare the introduction to the presentation, and the thanks for afterwards.

DVD recordings

Many funeral parlors have the facility of recording the service on a DVD, which is then presented to the family of the deceased. The funeral director will offer this service to the bereaved if it is available.

Memorabilia

If the deceased had a particular hobby, and many exhibits of it are in the family's keeping, some of these can also be placed on a table in the chapel or the foyer. Examples include sporting trophies, team clothing, sports equipment (e.g. fishing rods), carpentry, knitting, weaving, needlework, personal decorations, medals, awards and so on.

Conducting a special and professional service

The pain of loss and grief is great, so it is the role of a celebrant to put on record and pay tribute to the life that has been lived. Accordingly, the following is a guide to the preparation of the service, incorporating some 'must dos' which I have found helpful over the years.

Preparing the service

Most services I have conducted have had a time span of three to five days from the time of engagement. In this period, you have to make contact with the bereaved, carry out the initial interview, gather all the relevant information and write the service.

After receiving the appointment from the funeral director, it is therefore paramount that you make contact with the bereaved as soon as possible. There will be cases where the bereaved do not understand what is required to write and compose a service, so be frank with them about the amount of time you need to prepare a service that honours the deceased. See Chapter 2 for more information.

Revising and rewriting

The perfect service—is there such a thing? I would like to think that my services are true and meaningful portraits of the deceased but, without exception, when I replay them over in my mind, I always feel that there was some aspect that I could have done better. Letters and telephone calls from the family expressing their appreciation are most welcome, but I am always aware of the trust placed in me, and the work I had to do to deserve their thanks. So, without exception, after I have written a service, I revise, rewrite, revise and rewrite until satisfied.

I advise you to always ensure your services are of the highest quality. When you lose control over this, much of the personal feeling of a service is lost. An important part of this process is rewriting and revising everything you do. It's what all writers do, and it is as central to the success of your service as it is to the success of a novel or play or poem. I am constantly revising, even making changes right up to the day of the service, and even then I often cast my mind back and wish I could have made it even better.

Before the service

Being prepared before the service is very important so your duties run smoothly.

- Arrange your text on the lectern beforehand.

- Have a glass of water handy but out of sight.

- Check the music tapes or CDs have been supplied to the staff member controlling the audio equipment.

Checking name and date of birth

Before the service commences, consult the memorial sheet or book and double-check the deceased's full name and date of birth. It may seem unnecessary, but there have been occasions where these differ from what I have recorded when meeting with the family.

If there is a contradiction, you will need to quickly check with the funeral director. If the service held at a funeral parlour chapel, check with office staff, otherwise the funeral director may need to contact the office staff and compare records. This does happen—believe me!

Arrival of mourners

As the celebrant, you are not expected to escort mourners into the chapel or to the graveside. The funeral director will escort people to the waiting room if the funeral is at the chapel, or to graveside if at a cemetery.

However, I always make a point of greeting the family, as there may be last-minute changes to the ceremony that have not been conveyed to you or to the funeral director. It is paramount that you get everything right.

During the service

Commencement

When the mourners are seated, you can:

- walk from the entrance of the chapel, with the funeral director, down the aisle to the lectern/pulpit

- seat yourself near the lectern/pulpit prior to the commencement of the service.

This is a personal choice, or it may be governed by the shape and size of the premises where the service is being held.

I prefer walking down the aisle in the company of the funeral director. When walking down the aisle, see if you can both commence with your left foot. It sounds a little military in style, but it is just another aspect that will contribute to your air of professionalism.

After you have both bowed before the coffin, the funeral director will proceed to the pulpit/lectern where he will activate the microphone and then take his leave. You, as a celebrant, are now in charge and the success of the ceremony is in your hands.

If I do choose to take a seat next to the pulpit/lectern, I often walk the few steps to the main family members—those with whom you have arranged the service—and console them with a few kind words. This will also help the congregation feel that you care about the family and the deceased, and are showing your respect.

Conducting the service

You will find in Chapters 3–5 much detail about conducting the different stages of a funeral service. One thing to remember, though, is that when the going gets tough and solemnity is so evident, try sincerely for a light-hearted remark which will magically break the tension. Always remember: death does not put a ban on laughter and it is as acceptable to laugh as it is to cry.

For example, often in the course of delivering a eulogy I will ask if I have the correct pronunciation of a town, person or other name. Someone will always respond. I then say something like, 'And I've been practising that all night'. People often chuckle and feel more at ease. Other times, I will ask for a pet's name which I pretend I have forgotten.

Don't be afraid of including a bit of theatre in your service. It breaks down barriers and makes people feel more comfortable.

Concluding the service

Often there will be a burial committal after the service which takes place in the cemetery. When you have completed your dialogue and concluded with the benediction, the funeral director and staff will walk to the coffin. The funeral director will ask for pallbearers to come forward and for the mourners to stand while the coffin leaves the chapel. The family and mourners will be asked to follow the pallbearers.

When everyone is in place, you should lead the pallbearers and funeral staff down the aisle to the waiting hearse.

At a graveside burial, you should lead the pallbearers from the hearse to the graveside.

After the service

After the service—whether it is held at a funeral parlour, graveside, club or any other venue—always stay on. Keep in the background as you have done your job and the funeral director now should be the controller.

When the opportunity presents itself, give the family your best wishes and present them with a transcript of the service. Seek out and congratulate a speaker if they have done a good job. Thank any singers or musicians, including the organist, and funeral director and staff—particularly the staff member controlling the music or the recording of the service. These are just little things, but they are important.

Many times I have gone back to the refreshment room and served tea and coffee, even helped drying the dishes. You should feel a total involvement in the service—the little things mean a lot!

At a graveside funeral service, after the family and mourners have departed, but not before, you can pitch in to help the funeral staff to pack up. Many times I have got my hands dirty assisting with folding the mats, dismantling the marquee or packing up the chairs. It is important that you are a team player and have a total involvement in the service that you are conducting.

Asking for evaluation

In the aftermath of the service, I always reflect on the service with the funeral director, and ask whether any aspect should be reviewed for future services. I encourage them to share their honest opinions of my performance and have made considerable improvements because of advice received. My motto with any funeral director is that we are in our jobs together.

A funeral business is, in some ways, just like any other business. While a funeral director is providing an essential service, there is also a bottom line they have to meet. Just like any businesspeople, they will talk and focus on the number of services per annum and their market share.

Contacting the family

I usually wait one week before I pick up the phone and speak with the person that was the initial contact and on whose behalf I conducted the service. Without question, all appreciate my follow-up call. In some cases I have been able to suggest suitable reading material and even assistance if they are having trouble coping with their loss.

I'll never forget making such a call to the sister of a woman who had taken her own life. The living sister was very close to the deceased and her grieving was of urgent concern. I spoke with the doctor of both the deceased and her sister, and he took over. I believe he helped prevent what could have been a further tragedy.

Delivering a transcript

Often the service you have written and prepared as a transcript of the ceremony will be changed with last-minute requests. This often means that the transcript of the ceremony that you intended to present to the bereaved is no longer a true record of the service.

Explain this to the bereaved after the completion of the funeral service and convey to them that you will give them a true record when you have made the necessary changes. If the bereaved lives locally, you can drop off the transcript; however, if they live in a distant location an appropriate letter should accompany the revised transcript. The letter should be short and complimentary to those who attended and participated in the ceremony. Some examples follow.

Dear Angus,

As promised, enclosed is a copy of the service for Michael. What an excellent tribute your family and friends paid to him. So many people who I spoke to said such wonderful things about him—he was much loved.

Your eulogy was very special—one of the finest I have heard. I thank you for the privilege of conducting the service.

My thoughts are with you.

Dear Gwendoline,

As promised, enclosed is a copy of the service for Emily.

What a meaningful tribute was paid to Emily by her countless friends. The Town Hall had a wonderful atmosphere and ambience of love. In the reception room, people spoke of Emily to me with such high regard and with one of the greatest tributes one can have for another: respect.

Thank you for the privilege of conducting the service, which was very special to me.

Brightest blessings.

How much should a celebrant charge?

Without wishing to sound sanctimonious, I treat my role as a celebrant as a calling. If you are in it just for the money, you might as well give up now. You will not find your fortune here.

I have an agreement with the funeral parlours I work with, and they determine a suitable fee. We work together within three price ranges. There is a 'normal' fee, a 'budget' fee that is sometimes called for, and then there are those services that are necessarily free of charge. If I am contacted personally by the family or friends of the deceased, rather than the funeral parlour, I apply the same rules.

Don't despair, though—the majority of services do fit into the normal fee range, but many 'budget' fees are also called for. Free funeral services are usually saved for exceptional circumstances, but these do occasionally arise.

Above all, remember that *every* service you do should be performed with your heart and your mind, and to your full professional capacity. You should always conduct and deliver a service worthy of the deceased and the faith placed in you to do so.

I despair of celebrants who conduct services with such speed that they are virtually turning them out like sausages from a machine. One celebrant I encountered boasted to me that he often did three to four services a day, three or four days of the week, at the same crematorium—and mainly using the same material! As a celebrant, you should give those who have passed a meaningful, peaceful and unhurried farewell, and encourage the funeral directors and crematoriums you work with to show a similar respect.

Challenging situations for celebrants

When preparing and conducting funeral services, you will encounter many different situations with bereaved families and friends. Most of these encounters will be pleasant; some not so. However, as a celebrant you cannot be judgmental, and must always conduct the service with your normal civility, compassion and expertise.

Difficult family members or friends

There are insufficient words to soften the shock and pain we feel when someone close to us dies. People can feel a great range of emotions, and everyone grieves in their own way. Some display deep sorrow; some feel anger, blame, pain or hurt; some simply cannot believe this could happen to them; others are reluctant even to speak. The extreme nature of these expressions of grief can lead to mourners behaving in unpredictable ways.

Approving the service

On occasion, just before presenting the service, you may encounter a family member who wishes to see what you have written—not just the eulogy, but all the material. In most cases, I ask the person to trust me but there is always the exception.

One very difficult person insisted and, not wanting to add any further stress or hurt, I met with her prior to the service. We went through it together and not a reading or word was changed. Months later, the same person lost her other parent and she asked me to conduct the service—without going through the service word for word. I later found out that the person was not just thinking about the deceased, but what the family would think of her arrangement and choice of funeral director and celebrant. So it is good to remember that 'difficult' people often have good reason for being so.

Some in the profession believe that every transcript of the service should be viewed and approved prior to the service. Personally, I strongly disagree with this practice. If you have the confidence of the family, your delivery should not be impaired by hurried changes.

Gaining trust

To begin the process of talking with the bereaved, very early in the initial meeting or interview I express my sympathy and explain what part I will play in the service. I always ask for their co-operation and make them feel part of the process by saying that *together* we will write a lovely service for their departed loved one.

You will know very early in the meeting if you will have to work hard to gain the trust, confidence and acceptance of the bereaved. I can honestly say that I have overcome concerns by being natural, competent, caring and helpful. Sometimes just by being there, you will encourage the bereaved to talk. On occasions when a bereaved person is overcome with grief, and finds responses difficult, I have simply said, 'When you feel like telling me about it, I'd like to listen'.

Sharing memories with the grieving breaks down all barriers, and soon you will have some treasured memories that you can record and which will enable you to write a meaningful eulogy. I have laughed and cried with bereaved relatives and friends, embracing their grief and knowing that the healing process for them has begun.

Difficult situations at the service

At some services, you will need to draw on all your reserves of patience, calmness and professionalism. For example, one woman hated her husband so much that I had to refer to him throughout the service as 'the deceased', and was not allowed to mention

ner widow so disliked her deceased husband's family and friends that
, the only mourner. Instead of conducting the service from the pulpit I
me chapel services resemble the O.K. Corral, as family members seated
f the aisle stare daggers at each other.

On the odd occasion where a family member attends a service a little 'under the weather', it's best to leave other family members to control such occurrences.

Conducting funerals at short notice

On some occasions, instead of three to five days for preparation, you may only be able to meet with the bereaved 24 hours before the service. This provides little time to prepare the service, and I always endeavour to explain to the bereaved that I require a certain time to write a meaningful service for their lost loved one.

If such a short timeframe can't be avoided, you need to rely on your experience. When I first began as a celebrant I certainly could not have coped very well, but if you are properly organised you will find it easier. Have a range of readings, rituals, poetry, sayings and other material saved on your computer—this will give you resources at your fingertips if you need to prepare a service in a hurry.

If you are given several days' notice but cannot conduct the interview until 24 hours beforehand, you can at least make a start based on the type of funeral it is, and compile suitable readings from your records. Then, after you conduct the interview, you will have the maximum time to write the eulogy.

Last-minute changes

Most funeral directors will advise a family not to arrive until five minutes before the commencement of the service. In doing so, the funeral director's intention is to spare the families as many painful feelings as possible. However, such practice can be disconcerting to a celebrant, as often the family will have made various changes to the service among themselves which they will not have had a chance to convey to you. These might include alterations in the speakers, music, process for touching the coffin, flowers on the coffin, readings, prayers and so on.

As you can imagine, five minutes before the service commences doesn't leave you much time to make these changes. This situation calls for some hurried alterations to the script and will place you under some pressure. If you think the family may have some last-minute changes, a tip is to keep some blank pages in your prepared manuscript so you can record any new requests, such as another speaker, an extra reading or poem, additional or different music and so on.

I am of the opinion that the family should arrive at a reasonable time prior to the scheduled start, which allows time for the changes to be made and arranged. You may need to communicate this to the funeral director and/or the family beforehand, particularly when the changes may involve changes for the funeral staff as well. If the family do not wish to mingle with the mourners prior to the service they should be invited to wait in an anteroom or private area.

Repetition

This does occur, particularly in services for the aged. I have had the privilege of conducting many services for lovely elderly ladies and gentlemen. The eulogy is, of course, different at each funeral, but many of the meaningful readings that have stood the test of time and make for a wonderful service can be repeated. The only person that knows you are using the same format is you, and there are always one or two readings that can be substituted so the service feels fresh to you.

Services for babies do not occur as often, but if you have prepared a satisfactory service you can refer to those notes to help you write another service (see Chapter 10).

Services for people who have taken their own lives are difficult, too, and I always refer to past notes if appropriate. I sincerely hope that in your life as a funeral celebrant you do not have to conduct services for people who have been murdered. They have occurred in my time, however, and again you may feel that using some of the same material is called for (see Chapter 9).

Pronouncing difficult names

The method I use to make sure I don't pronounce a name incorrectly during a service is to spell out the name phonetically in my notes. This has never let me down. In the transcript of the service that I present to the family the names are, of course, spelled the correct way,

So, for example, in once instance I made a note that the surname *Ehrenfeld* was pronounced *Air-en-feld*; in another, that *Harberecht* was pronounced *Har-bright*, and so on. This is particularly important in the region I work in, where the families come from a wide range of cultural backgrounds. One town in my region, for example, was the stepping-off place for many migrant families in the 1940s and 1950s. In another nearby town, there is a large population of German people who came to the region to establish vineyards.

The same applies for hard-to-pronounce places of birth, but you can take certain liberties with this. If a person was born in a town in the Netherlands with a name that is very difficult to pronounce, for instance, you could simply say the person was born in the Netherlands. Most families, when you discuss this action with them, will agree.

Children at funerals

Children need to say their goodbyes too, and should be encouraged (not forced) to share the funeral experience and attend the funeral of a loved one. The death of a loved one affects everyone in the family, including children, so they should not be left out.

On many occasions I have conducted the interview with the family with children present. I believe children realise the solemnity of the loss of a loved one and they can take comfort from taking part in the family's mourning and not being excluded.

Distractions can occur at funeral services when a baby is crying or a child is displaying unruly behaviour. Often the parent will leave the chapel or graveside if a baby's crying is excessive. For older children, most funeral parlors have toys or lollies which they can offer to distract the child.

Unusual locations

It helps to be prepared for anything! The bereaved choose locations for funeral services that are important to them or to the deceased, so it is important to respect the family's wishes, no matter what your personal preference.

Mourners' private homes, church halls, Masonic halls, town halls, RSL clubs, sporting clubs, golf clubs, a football ground (between the goalposts), a cricket ground (on the pitch), a racecourse, a tennis court, a darts club, an engineering company, a fire station, a private airstrip, a horse stud, a lake, a winery and a pub are just some of the places I have conducted services in. The mourners gathered in the pub didn't have far to go for a drink after the service ended!

Some churches do not allow civil celebrants to conduct services in them; in these cases you may have to perform the service in an adjacent hall.

Odd or unexpected events

No two services are alike, so always expect the unexpected. It is important to realise that the service belongs not only to the deceased but also to the bereaved, so accept the unexpected and maintain your professionalism, no matter what happens.

Imagine the scene: it is a graveside service and burial in a rural cemetery. A local identity has passed—a real wag and raconteur. He loved a beer or two (or three) and had requested that such refreshments be made available because he did not want people standing around with long faces. A solemn occasion became a rather boisterous celebration. The funeral staff and I had to wait for all to depart before we tidied the grave site, packed up and departed, as the wake extended long after sunset.On another occasion the deceased, a caterer, left the instruction that his farewell at the graveside must be catered for, with only the best food. It was! And yes, the funeral director and staff all stayed to enjoy it.

In the next chapter you'll find out more about conducting interviews—a very important stage that allows you to capture the life, character and essence of a person in the service you prepare.

PART
2

Preparing the Service

2 *The interview: creating a portrait*

First impressions are vitally important for any meeting with new people, but they are especially so for a funeral celebrant meeting a bereaved family or friends. You are effectively a stranger coming into their lives and asking for very personal information at a time when they feel incredibly vulnerable and upset. If you are able to win their trust with your professionalism and offer sincere empathy, however, then you will be able to gather a wealth of information to help you to prepare an appropriate service.

In this chapter we'll look at the different aspects of these meetings, including:

- your role as the celebrant

- the questions you need to ask and the information you need to collect

- the information about your own services you should impart.

The celebrant's role

I consider the initial meeting to be the most important aspect of my role as a funeral celebrant. Sure, you have to write a professional service and sure, you have to deliver a high-quality service, but the first encounter with the family allows you to share in their suffering and grief. This is *always* a significant part of your role, but especially so in passings involving suicides, tragic accidents, children and babies.

You will have to carefully balance a number of roles when interviewing the bereaved: grief counsellor, information-gatherer and organiser. I actually recommend that all civil celebrants acknowledge this responsibility by undertaking some training in grief counselling. It will give you some understanding of how to comfort and listen to the bereaved in an empathetic and sensitive way.

This is a very delicate time for all concerned. Grieving people are so often strangers to the emotions they are feeling; their lives and thoughts may be in utter turmoil. They will not be familiar with the process of arranging a funeral, so it is up to you as the celebrant to set the scene and take the lead. Your aim should be to conduct a pleasant, sincere, helpful, fact-finding interview that will set the bereaved at ease and culminate in a special service for their lost loved one.

Making initial contact

When making initial contact with the bereaved and organising a first meeting, encourage them to invite as many family and friends to the meeting as possible. This gives you a much broader view of the deceased's life, not just a one-sided story, and will help you to bring a depth and reality to your eulogy.

Every passing has its own unique circumstances, so it makes sense that the situations bereaved friends and family will find themselves in are also unique. So it's natural that even in the process of meeting the bereaved, you will have to be incredibly flexible. If you're able to meet the bereaved in their own home, this can help them to feel comfortable at the initial consultation, but meetings can take place in any number of different locations and circumstances. Don't judge—just be adaptable.

Meeting the bereaved

I treat every interview with the bereaved as a healing time for them. Inviting them to talk about the person they have lost is a way of helping them with the natural grieving process.

Breaking the ice

After pleasantries are exchanged, it can be helpful to make some polite small talk—comment on some features of the house or garden, for instance, or the view, or any other topic that comes easily. If children are present, ask their names. Admiring a baby can be an easy way to break the ice. It's important to put the bereaved at ease.

It's okay to ask, even before being invited to sit, how the deceased came to pass, and whether it had been sudden or following a longer struggle.

Gathering information

Don't feel locked into a strict order of questions—try to let the interview flow naturally. Later in the chapter you'll find a list of all the important information that you should collect, but there is no need to rigidly follow a set format.

Be flexible and record answers and anecdotes as they're offered, however, be careful to ensure that all questions are answered. Often a question near the end of your list will be referred to early in the natural flow of conversation, so record that answer as it arises and bypass the question when you come to it on your list. In my list of questions, one of the final ones is where the person passed—whether it was at home, in medical care or elsewhere—but often I will discover the answer in the first few minutes of a discussion.

If things become a little strained at any point, it can be helpful to change the direction of the conversation. Perhaps you could pleasantly ask about the hobbies and interests of the deceased. Such a question will often be answered with a barrage of information, as the bereaved can set aside the details of death for a few moments and recall some fond memories. All of this information is valuable for you to record.

Sometimes you may only end up mentioning the deceased's virtues and achievements, or even exaggerating them; human failings that cannot be mentioned without unkindness may be forgotten in the final service. Nonetheless, you should aim to piece together a solid background understanding of the deceased through the interview, even if you do not use all the information you have gathered.

Concluding the meeting

Make sure you don't leave without offering the bereaved your business card, and saying 'Ring me if you think of anything else'. At such an emotional time, grieving loved ones can easily forget to offer important information. In many cases, the interview has just stirred the pot, and family members will think of more things when you have left, or will talk with those not at the interview so that everyone has an input into what they would like included in the eulogy. Suggest they contact you by phone or email if there is anything else that they wish to have included in the service, or anything you can do to help.

Always leave the family with some compassionate words. It's a good feeling to leave knowing that they have confidence in you to conduct a memorable and meaningful service for their departed loved one.

Rechecking details

When you arrive home and start to draw together your ideas for the service, you may find that you have forgotten to ask a pertinent point, such as the deceased's date of birth, or one of the parent's names. These small details can often be quickly found out by ringing the funeral director so as not to disturb the bereaved again.

Of course, there are many other details—such as the name of a brother, sister or friend—that the funeral director won't be able to help you with. If you missed one of these you'll have to make contact again. Do this cheerfully by phoning the relevant family member. Simply say that in the hustle and bustle of the interview you forget to ask. Often the bereaved will offer some more information to you as well, having had time after the initial interview to think about the life of their departed loved one.

You might think that forgetting an obvious and important detail at the first interview is an absolute no-no, but in reality it happens easily—particularly when you have many family members and friends all contributing to the interview. The result can be a joyful chaos which can form one of the first steps in the bereaved's healing process. I have come away from such meetings with my head ringing but, amazingly, have found that it all comes together into a meaningful service.

Meeting at a funeral parlour

At times it will be more convenient to arrange an interview at a funeral parlour. This may be your home territory and as such it's important to put the bereaved at ease in these unfamiliar surroundings. Funeral parlours usually have a comforting ambience about them, which often helps to ease the process of the initial meeting.

Offer a cup of tea or coffee and biscuits prior to commencing the interview. If the funeral director has not done so, offer to show the bereaved the chapel and the refreshment room if they are having some refreshments after the service.

Telephone meetings

Sometimes it's necessary to conduct an interview with the bereaved via telephone. This often happens when, due to distance, you are unable to meet personally with the bereaved.

In these cases, after the initial pleasantries and expression of sorrow, you will be able to use and refer to the question sheet included at the end of this chapter quite easily without drawing attention to it. But I miss the personal touch that you receive from a personal meeting. It's much easier to gauge the depth of the bereaved's sorrow and their affinity with the deceased when you meet face to face, and it can be more difficult to draw out some light-hearted stories and anecdotes over the phone.

A repeat call by either party is often necessary before you are satisfied that the information you have collated will enable you to write a meaningful service.

How much time should you allow?

It's impossible to name a figure that will accurately sum up the time required for an initial interview. In my experience, it's a mistake to even attempt putting a timeframe on it. Spend as long as it takes to record the information you need to draft a meaningful ceremony. Remember that the service should reflect the unique nature of the person whose life is being honoured.

I have sat with families for hours until I was confident that I could leave them, knowing that they had confidence in me to compose and conduct a beautiful service about their lost loved one. I have also attended initial interviews with families that were just going through the motions and could not bring the interview to a close soon enough. Perhaps there was not much love or respect for the deceased, or perhaps they were detached and numbed by their grief. Whatever the case, it is your role to ensure that enough information is gathered to create a meaningful service—no matter what the circumstances are.

What questions should you ask?

With so many facts, names and memories coming out at an interview, it can be easy to lose track of the outcome that you need to achieve by the end of the meeting. As we mentioned earlier, while it's important to be flexible and to allow an interview to be sidetracked if the bereaved are finding the process difficult, it can also be helpful to have a checklist of facts you need to collect to write a comprehensive, meaningful and accurate service. A checklist allows you to:

- follow whatever direction the bereaved lead you and yet quickly return to check any gaps in your information

- jog your own memory, ensuring you remember to ask for the pertinent information.

So, let's go through some of the important facts you'll need to gather, then look at an example checklist you might find useful.

Names and nicknames

Naturally, you should find out the deceased's full name, but also be sure to include any nicknames. Seek guidance as to the preferred name to use throughout the service. For example, it's important to differentiate between names and preferred nicknames, such as:

- Ronald, Ron or Ronnie

- Robert, Rob, Bob, Bobby or Robbie

- Joseph or Joe

- Albert, Bert or Al

- Florence or Flo

- Elizabeth, Lizbeth, Betty, Beth or Libby

- Marg, Marge, Margie, Meg, Peg, Peggy or Margaret.

You should explain to the bereaved that, even if a nickname is preferred, it is necessary at the formal beginning of the service to use the person's full given name. In some cases it may be appropriate to alternate between a nickname and full name at different times in the service.

If a nickname is not widely used, or was only used amongst certain circles, then some mourners may be puzzled by the use of this name and feel a little put-out if they have never known the deceased by that name. Aim to bypass any confusion at the beginning of your service by referring to the correct full name in your opening remarks, and follow this by mentioning that the deceased was also affectionately known to some by a nickname. Repeat this procedure when you deliver the eulogy (see example in Chapter 4).

Age and birth details

Of course, you need to find out the deceased's age and date of birth. These particulars can easily be uncovered by contacting the funeral director, however.

The town, city and country of birth are also relevant facts to find out. If the pronunciation of a place name is difficult, you can write it down phonetically in your notes so that you pronounce it correctly (see examples in Chapter 5). Double-check the pronunciation you have written down with the family members.

Service particulars

Next, it's relevant to get some of the service particulars out of the way. For example, you'll need to find out, or confirm:

- who the funeral director is

- where the service will be conducted

- the date and time of the service

- whether a cremation or graveside burial, or both, will be performed.

Of course, these details are of vital planning importance—not just for the practical reason of finding out where you will need to be and when, but also to understand something of the atmosphere in which the service will be held.

Names of family members

It's often useful to remind yourself that you're conducting a service for the deceased's friends and family, so it's important to collect their details and correctly refer to them in the stories you collect.

- Parents' names are a good place to start. Often first names will suffice. Ascertain whether the deceased's parents are still living or deceased and, if living, whether they will attend the service.

- Other family members—brothers, sisters, husbands, wives, children and grandchildren—should all be recognised.

- Partners are obviously very important characters in the deceased's story. It can be helpful to tell some of the story of their meeting. Find out where and how they met and when and where they were married. If there is no marriage but a long-term partner, then ask appropriate questions.

- Grandchildren and great-grandchildren should also be listed, however in some cases there are so many that even the family suggest that numbers only be mentioned. It's also nice to ascertain what affectionate names they used for the deceased—Grandpa, Granddad, Pa, Pop, Nana, Nan, Nonna, Grandma and so on.

These days many services are for people who married more than once, or had more than one long-term partner. They may also have children and stepchildren. In these cases it's important to establish with compassion whether the bereaved are comfortable mentioning previous relationships. You can ask, 'How would you like me to handle this?' Be guided by their instruction as to how you refer to previous partners.

Names of friends

Of course, friends are often just as important—sometimes more so—than family. It may be that there are one or two very special friends who deserve a special mention for the place they had in the life of the deceased. Whenever I ask about friends, though, I always preface my question by saying one must be careful in this respect, as the deceased may have countless friends, and if only a few are mentioned others may be hurt.

Education and early years

Often it can be useful to start to paint a picture of the deceased by looking back at their early years and moving forward. In this case it can be helpful to find out about their schooling. Ask about their primary and secondary schools and any later studies.

Find out what qualifications were attained and what goals and aspirations the deceased had when growing up and going through school. You might also ask about their early life and encourage some interesting stories.

Occupation and interests

For many of us, our occupation shapes how we spend a lot of our time and who we are. Find out the deceased's trade, profession or occupation. You should also ask about hobbies or interests that may have shaped their personality. These might include reading, gardening, arts, music, television, radio, theatre, nature, travel, animals, flying, fishing or anything specific to their own lives and loves.

Community connections

Many people are best known and remembered in the wider community through various community groups, clubs and service organisations. If this is the case, it will be important to include some details of this in the service as a large number of the mourners may have known the deceased through this connection.

For example, the deceased might have passionately supported—or even played with—a local sports team (football, soccer, rugby, netball or cricket). Many coffins are draped with a football, soccer or rugby jumper, and it's not unusual to have a club theme song played during the service.

Alternatively, the person may have been a member of a Lions, Rotary, Apex, Freemasonry or Probus club, or a similar community group. Or, if the deceased completed military service, it may be through a local RSL club that the deceased was most connected to the community. Find out the details of any military service or club/community positions held.

Personal characteristics

After establishing something of a rapport with the bereaved, ask them to describe the deceased. This can lead to a few light-hearted episodes that are recalled and worth repeating in the service if they'll bring back fond memories for those in attendance. Search for any relevant personal information that the bereaved consider important and that they would like you to emphasise.

Find out whether the deceased was known for any memorable habits—either good or bad. This type of question can also lead to some humorous stories. He or she may have been a passionate supporter of a political party, smoked too much or had other well-known vices. There may be a favourite pet that was never far from the person's side, a musical instrument they played or a love of nature that helps define the deceased's personal characteristics in the minds of many.

Discussing the service

Rather than stick to a set formula for the service, I like to discuss ideas with the bereaved and allow them to suggest different formats or elements that might help make the service even more memorable.

Music

Music can play an important role in creating an appropriate atmosphere. Although the funeral director may have already discussed this aspect of the service with the bereaved, you will often find that the final selection is made in consultation with you.

If the deceased was a music fan, the family and friends will know some favourite pieces. However, if the deceased was not interested in music, the family can choose music they find comforting. If they need assistance then I'm always happy to suggest appropriate music—see Chapter 1 for some suggestions. It's handy to have a few ideas that you can fall back on if they're called for. Some families prefer organ music and this can be arranged in conjunction with the funeral director.

Other speakers

I have found that very early in the interview it will usually be established whether a family members or friends would like to speak at the service. As the eulogy is the central part and heart of the service, a personal tribute from those who have an intimate knowledge of the deceased is a great asset.

In many cases the family will be happy for you to present a eulogy, however you always need to encourage others to share their thoughts. If other speakers will be presenting, be sure to record their names so you can introduce them appropriately in the service.

In my experience, it is worthwhile to encourage family and friends to take part in the service. See Chapter 3 for suggested examples of readings for children and grandchildren.

In many cases, family members who wish to speak have doubts about their ability to get through a eulogy, reading and poems without breaking up. I suggest to them that their words are written out so as I can take over if this occurs. In some cases I suggest the words are read in tandem, with each speaker providing strength and support to the other. This procedure is especially recommended when young children wish to speak.

Suggesting readings

I always carry with me some sample readings that demonstrate the love of a wife for her lost husband, a son or daughter for their deceased mother or father, grandchildren for their grandparents and dear friends for each other. These can be offered to the appropriate person if they are not able to come up with their own words. They may even find they are unable to perform a public reading and they may wish for you, as the celebrant, to read on their behalf.

Let's say that in the course of interview you establish that there are people amongst the bereaved who are capable of speaking about their loved one, but are too overcome with grief to compose a tribute. In such cases you can delve into your briefcase and find something to offer them as a reading.

Reflection time

You should explain that a few minutes of reflection time is usually included in each service. This allows everyone to observe a few moments of silence to reflect in their thoughts or a private prayer on the meaning of the life of the deceased person to them. This can also take place while music is played.

In addition, reflection time might include a reading of 'The Lord's Prayer' or other scripture readings or religious rites as appropriate. A photo or slide show presentation might also be included, or appropriate memorabilia might be shown as a focus for the reflection. Ideas for an appropriate reflection period should be discussed with the bereaved at the interview.

Refreshments

It is fairly customary for refreshments to be served after the service, allowing the deceased's family and friends to gather in a less formal environment and comfort each other, swap stories and share memories.

You might like to discuss this with the bereaved at the interview. Ideally, you should be able to announce in your introductory remarks that refreshments will be served after the conclusion of the service—whether at the funeral parlour, a club, a hall or someone's home if that is the case.

Order of service

Whether or not to have a printed order of service is a personal choice of the family. To many it is a memorial and record of this solemn occasion applicable to their lost loved one. If hymns are to be sung, an order of service is necessary so that people can follow the words of the hymns.

Generally, the order of service should be kept simple and comprise a two-page (A4 folded) document. Other designs, such as bookmarks and greeting card-sized documents, are also becoming popular. Collect examples of these documents and take them with you to your interviews with the bereaved.

I usually offer my experience to assist in the wording and design of the document, but it should be the task of the funeral director rather than the celebrant to arrange and print the orders of service. In other cases, a computer-literate member of the family will prepare the document and give it to the funeral director for duplication.

Here are some ideas for what to include on the order of service.

Front page

The front page can be headed with words such as 'A Service of Celebration and Thanksgiving' or 'In Loving Memory of', with the full name of the deceased. A photo can be centred on the page, and the dates of birth and passing can be centred at the bottom of the page

Page 2

The second page should outline the order of service, for example:

1   Celebrant's name

2   Introduction (by celebrant)

3   Readings

4   Eulogy (by members of family, friend or celebrant)

5   Tribute by others

6   Audiovisual presentation (e.g. PowerPoint)

7   Reflection (a reading or a music selection)

8   'The Lord's Prayer' (if requested)

9   Committal

10   Final tribute (music selection)

11   Benediction

Page 3

The third page can contain an appropriate reading. One short, poignant reading is 'Love doesn't end with dying', reproduced in Chapter 2.

Page 4

The final page expresses appreciation from the family of bereaved to those attending the funeral service. For example:

> *The family of Anthony would like to thank you for your presence here today, and for the love and support which has been shown to them.*
>
> *You are invited to join with the family after the service to remember Anthony and share in some refreshments at the Harmouth Bowling Club.*

The final magic question

Out of habit I like to finish an interview with the bereaved by asking, 'What will you most miss about the deceased?' It's a simple question but the answers can provide the essential theme for the service.

Interview checklist

The following is a checklist you can use during your fact-finding interviews. It contains a list of questions, from which I record details. As I have indicated above, it is by no means exhaustive and it's not always possible to ask questions in order, but it's a useful guide and can help you to make sure you have a sound base of information.

Table 1 Interview checklist

SERVICE FOR: [Name]	
Place and date:	
Funeral parlour:	
Burial, cremation or both:	
Date:	Time:
CONTACT FOR BEREAVED	
Name:	
Address:	
Email:	Phone:
BIRTH DETAILS	
Date:	Age:
Place:	
HUSBAND/WIFE/PARTNER	
Name:	
Where met:	Date:
Where married:	Date:
FRIENDS AND RELATIVES	
Parents:	
Brothers:	
Sisters:	
Children and their partners:	

Grandchildren:
Great-grandchildren:
Special friends attending:

SCHOOLING (NAMES AND LOCATIONS)

Primary:
Secondary:
Tertiary:
Other qualifications:

OCCUPATION(S)

HOBBIES/INTERESTS/ACHIEVEMENTS

WAR SERVICE

Yes / No	Details:
RSL, National Service, Legacy, other (give details):	

LIKES AND DISLIKES

GOOD & BAD HABITS

DETAILS OF PASSING

Home/hospital/other:

Thanks to relevant carers:

OTHER RELEVANT DETAILS

SERVICE PARTICULARS

Music:

Ideas:

Images:

Videos, photos, PowerPoint or other audiovisual presentations:

Flowers:

SPECIAL READINGS/PRAYERS

OTHER SPEAKERS

REFRESHMENTS

Where and when:

Offering service suggestions

If the bereaved are too overcome with grief or not ready to discuss the life of the deceased, it may be helpful to leave them a list of the questions above, along with the following service suggestions, for them to consider in their own time.

1   It is appropriate to play music before the commencement of the service. This might be the funeral parlour's tranquil background music or music of your choice. If a graveside service is requested, a portable player can be used.

2   Spoken tributes from loved ones are wonderful, but they are not easy to deliver. It is a good idea to write or type out speeches or readings so that if the speaker falters, the celebrant can take over until the speaker has regained composure. Sometimes participants in tandem can support each other. This is a good idea with young children or teenagers.

3   Whether or not this is a religious service, you may feel it is appropriate to say a prayer or perform other religious rites. If you desire them, please specify what prayers should be included and I will always introduce by saying, 'Those of you who wish to, please join with me in saying a prayer.'

4   There will be some silent reflection time in the service. During this time, music of your choice can be played or an appropriate reading made.

5   There will be time for tributes by family members and loved ones, where you may come forward and touch the casket or place a flower on it.

6   Photos and special memorabilia can be placed on a table at the front of the chapel to represent a life's journey. A stand can be supplied by the funeral parlour and set up in the foyer.

7   An announcement about refreshments after the service can be made to give everyone somewhere to meet up. This may be at the funeral parlour, a family residence, local club or any venue you choose.

As you read on, we will begin our exploration of how you can take the information gathered at the interview and create a meaningful service. We'll start at the very beginning and look at writing an opening to a service in the next chapter.

3 The opening: setting the tone

The opening of a service is a crucial part of a funeral service as it sets the tone and pace for what is to follow. It's important to set mourners at ease from the very beginning and to capture the character of the deceased for grieving loved ones.

In the previous section we addressed the process of visiting the family and compiling all the relevant information to enable you to write a caring and meaningful service. Now, in this chapter, we're going to look at the process for writing an opening to a service.

Often a prayer or meaningful verse—particularly anything that was a favourite of the deceased or the bereaved—helps to set the tone. While a selection of appropriate examples are included in this chapter, there are many more that you might choose. The key is to make sure you establish an appropriate tone and character for the personality and life of the deceased.

Introducing yourself

As the service opens you will be faced with the question of whether or not you wish to introduce yourself overtly to the congregation. I believe that this is an individual choice that depends on your own feelings, the service your are conducting and the circumstances.

If there is an order of service booklet produced then your name is likely to be printed, so there is no reason to repeat who you are if you don't wish to do so. I also believe that there is no need to introduce myself from a marketing point of view. If you have performed well, you will soon become known and your services requested in the community without needing to make announcements during each service.

If you do wish to introduce yourself, a simple introduction at the beginning of the service is appropriate, such as:

> *Good morning, and welcome to the funeral service for ----*.*

> *My name is Barry Young, and I am a civil celebrant and funeral celebrant. It's my privilege to be conducting this service for ---- today.*

* Where the name of the deceased person is to be inserted, you will see four dashes ---- in the text.

An opening reading

An opening verse is a great way to create a feeling of comfort and to set the tone for the service. I try to begin my services with some meaningful words prior to the main introduction. One of my favourite opening verses that never seems to fail is:

> *Love doesn't end with dying,*
> *Or leave in the last breath.*
>
> *For someone you've loved deeply,*
> *Love doesn't end with death.*
>
> *Author unknown*

Another lovely verse I use for setting the tone is:

> *I ask not wealth, nor length of days*
> *Nor pride nor power, nor worldly praise.*
>
> *But just a little quiet place where a friend may come,*
> *Laying their hand on the door as though it were home.*
>
> *Author unknown*

You might even augment this type of verse with something a little philosophical along these lines:

> *May we have the serenity to accept the things we cannot change,*
> *courage to change the things we can, and wisdom to know the*
> *difference.*

Another appropriate poem is 'There is no Night Without a Dawning' by Helen Steiner Rice.

In this way it's possible to piece together any number of appropriate verses or inspirational words. Of course, each service should be tailored to the individual who has passed, but with a little experience you will soon find that this is reasonably easy to do once you have a collection of readings, verses and inspirational words to draw upon.

A simple opening is often the best—there is less room for error or thoughts that don't ring true amongst the bereaved, and the mourners will be able to contemplate their own thoughts rather than digest a long or complicated reading.

Light-hearted verses

Some characters are so full of life that even in death it seems as though something would be missing if you couldn't find room for a light-hearted reading and celebration in their service.

There is a short, wonderful, witty poem written by the entertainer and comedian Joyce Grenfell, called 'If I Should Go Before the Rest of You' which is an ideal fit for reminding mourners of the deceased's love of life and optimism under any circumstances.

If you start with a more light-hearted reading, it is a good idea to follow it up with something like:

> *You might think that is a very light-hearted way to commence a*
> *funeral service, but that is what ---- would have wanted. This is not*
> *only a funeral service, but a celebration of a meaningful life lived by*
> *a wonderful, fun-loving person.*

Opening verses for elderly people

Let's look at some words that are appropriate to open a service for an elderly lady, then one that is more fitting for an elderly gentleman's passing, and finally one which could be used for either an elderly man or woman.

An elderly lady

They say it's a beautiful journey
From the old world to the new.
Someday we'll all take that journey,
Up the stairway that leads to you.

And when we reach that garden
Where all are free from pain,
We'll put our arms around you, ----,
And we'll never part again.

For God looked around his garden,
And found an empty space,
Then He looked upon the Earth,
And found a lady full of grace.

A golden heart stopped beating,
Two hands were laid to rest.
The garden must be beautiful,
Because He only takes the best.

Author unknown

An elderly gentleman

In a sea-blue harbour, two ships sailed. One was setting off on a voyage; the other was coming home to port.

Everyone cheered at the ship going out, but the ship sailing in was hardly noticed.

To this, a wise man said, 'Do not rejoice over a ship setting out to sea, for you cannot know what terrible storm it may endure.

'Rejoice over the ship that has safely reached its port and brings its passengers home in peace.

'And this is the way of the world. When a child is born, we all rejoice; when someone dies we all grieve.

'But you and I, we should do the opposite. For none of us can tell what trials and tribulations await the newborn child.'

So, when a love ones dies in peace, we should rejoice, for ---- has completed a long, meaningful and worthwhile journey.

An elderly man or woman

In the rising of the sun and in its going down,
We will remember him.

In the beginning of the year and when it ends,
We will remember him.

When we notice the things he liked,
We will remember him.

When we see in others glimpses of his ways,
We will remember him.

When we see in ourselves things that he would value,
We will remember him.

When we see the example that he set and the difference that he made,
We will remember him.

So as long as we live,
He too will live as we remember him.

Today is a closing and an opening,
A saying goodbye and a saying hello again.

So while we say farewell to the ---- we knew,
We greet the ---- who has become so much part of us,
The ---- who lives on with us,
In the thoughts and memories that we will cherish forever.

Adapted from the Litany of Remembrance

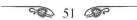

Here is another adaptation along a similar theme.

When we are weary and in need of strength,
When we are lost and sick at heart,
We will remember you, ----.

When we have a joy we crave to share,
When we have decisions that are difficult to make,
When we have achievements that are based on [his/hers],
We will remember you, ----.

At the blowing of the wind and in the chill of winter,
At the opening of the buds and in the rebirth of Spring,
We will remember you, ----.

At the blueness of the skies and in the warmth of summer,
At the rustling of the leaves and in the beauty of autumn,
We will remember you, ----.

At the rising of the sun and at its setting,
We will remember you, ----.

As long as we live, you too will live,
For you are now a part of us,
As we remember you, ----.

Adapted from the Litany of Remembrance

Opening verses for tragic circumstances

Many services are imbued with extreme grief and sadness—the deaths of young people, tragic accidents, suicides and so on. Sometimes the mood of deep grief will be so intense that you might begin the service by asking for courage and strength and for everyone to bond together and help each other through their pain.

> *There is no doubt today we all need strength to get through this tragic loss of life. The following verse is a way of seeking that strength and comfort that will help us get through this service together.*
>
> *Within us is the strength to meet life's challenges.*
> *We are stronger than we think.*
>
> *Every challenge in our life helps us to grow.*
> *Every problem we encounter strengthens our mind and our soul.*
>
> *Every trouble we overcome increases our understanding of life.*
> *When all our troubles weigh heavily on our shoulders,*
> *Remember that beneath the burden we can stand tall.*
>
> *Because we are never given more than we can handle,*
> *And we are stronger than we think.*
>
> *So we can do this together today, can't we?*
>
> *Adapted from Lisa Wroble, 'Within you is the strength to meet life's challenges'*

The introduction

Once you have completed your opening verse you will need to make some introductory remarks to simply outline the procedure and the purpose of the day's ceremony.

At this point there are obviously any number of different words you might use. The following is an example that expresses the necessary sentiments and provides the bereaved with the information they need before you launch into the introduction.

> *As you are aware, a fine gentleman has been lost to us. And we are here today to celebrate the life of ---- [full name]. And I ask that you please feel free to be at one with your sorrow, your sadness, your grief and your memories—but also I ask you to feel the gladness, the happiness, the purpose and the serenity of a life so well lived.*

It is then be worth explaining the procedure for after the funeral. Usually a wake will have been organised—a simple gathering of mourners, perhaps at someone's home or in a room at the funeral parlour, or a club, hall or other local facility. A simple cup of tea and a chat can be a wonderful tonic and provide relief for many of the mourners. It is a time for them to bond together, remember the deceased and share their grief.

In continuing the introduction the following may be appropriate:

> *I thank you all for your presence here today, as we commemorate with sorrow but also with respect, joy and thankfulness the life of ----.*

> *After the completion of the service here at the Willis Chapel, the cortege will leave for North Kinglea Cemetery, where the commital will take place. At the conclusion of the committal ceremony you are invited to the Supper Room at the Kinglea RSL Club for a cuppa, a chat and to recollect the special times you spent with ----.*

> *Death, in a number of ways, unites us all, for it demands that each of us put aside our toil, our business and our pleasures to unite ourselves with everyone here—fellow mourners—who share in a common bond of love and respect for the deceased.*

> *As with any funeral service, we gather to mourn a departed loved one, to pay tribute to their achievements and their life, to comfort one another and give our support to each other. We can feel a great range of emotions—anger, pain, hurt, sorrow and grief—but there is one*

*thing that cannot be taken away and that is the experience of loving
and the experience of friendship.*

*When we lose someone dear to us, the hurt can be almost unbearable,
yet somehow we seem to get through it. And I believe that it is
because we feel such pain—because the inner ache is so great—that
the grief and heartache we feel bears witness to the depths of our love.*

*You see, grief is a great indicator and measure of love. It simply
cannot and does not exist except where there has been love.*

An elderly person

Of course, as with every part of the service, it is appropriate to tailor the opening to
suit the particular circumstances. For example, if it's an elderly man or woman, you
might add:

*And I am sure that ---- would not want you to grieve in hurt or pain,
but grieve in the joy that she has given, that she has received and that
she has shared.*

*And so it is in thinking of ---- and saying goodbye for the time being
we can say thank you to ---- and celebrate a life well lived.*

A young person

If the service is for a young person, you might instead say something along the following lines:

When we lose someone dear to us, the hurt can be almost unbearable. Yet the hurt inside gives us a strange comfort—it is telling us just how much we loved them.

I believe that it is because we feel such pain—because the inner ache is so great—that we realise how much we loved. The grief and heartache we feel bears witness to the depths of our love.

You see, grief is a great indicator and measure of love. It simply cannot and does not exist except where there has been love.

So it is in thinking of ---- today and saying goodbye for the time being that we can say thank you to ---- for what [he/she] has given us.

----'s passing has left a deep sadness in our lives. This time we spend together today is to remember ----. It is also to allow our sorrow and sadness to surface and be expressed in words, or tears, or reflection, or in whatever way is meaningful to each of us.

Our being together here is a support and comfort for each of us, whether a member of the family or a caring friend. Our collective sorrow and grief becomes a collective strength enabling us to find closure and move on without the physical presence of our beloved ----. Let us remember ----'s life with gratitude, joy, gladness and love.

Thank you for your presence here today, united in strength and love.

A middle-aged person

You might try another angle again for a middle-aged father and parent taken in the prime of his life.

We are here today because ----, husband, father and friend, has found the comfort of contentment and peace.

On behalf of [names of people who arranged the service], I thank you for your presence here today as we commemorate with sorrow but also with joy and thankfulness the life of ----.

We grieve today with thoughts of ---- foremost in our minds. His passing has brought sorrow to his family and friends, particularly as the ties of love and friendship were so strong.

But while we think of ----'s passing with sadness and regret, we should recall his life with respect and happiness.

You see, nothing can detract from the happiness and closeness you shared with ----. Nothing can affect the happiness and the joy of life that ---- knew. Nothing can affect your love for him and his love for you.

Family and friends can never be altered by time, circumstance or even by death. The past, with all its meaning, is sacred and secure.

Be grateful that ---- was part of your lives and let his influence—his character, his warmth and his deeds—live on.

When there are few mourners

Sometimes there will be occasions where the deceased has no family or friends to speak of at the service. In this case it is still important to find a way to give comfort to the few people who are present. The following words may fit the occasion:

> *While we grieve today because we are parting with someone we have known and cared for, we are also faced with the fact that we do not mourn alone. At this time, thousands of others are mourning the loss of their loved ones too.*
>
> *Many of these people have died in peace, at the end of full and useful lives. Many have died middle-aged in the prime of their lives, and many have died young, needlessly. Others have died defending a cause, and many have seen their loved ones torn from them by the awful results of man's inhumanity to man.*
>
> *We only have to glance at our newspapers today to realise that there is much heartache in the world today and, bearing in mind the sorrows that others are experiencing today, we come to realise that we are living in a larger world than our own, and that the best way to face the unavoidable fact of death and parting is to take upon our shoulders the troubles of others—to go on caring so that we may help to remove the injustice and preventable sorrow in this world.*
>
> *I am sure that is what ---- would want from us.*

Thoughts on life and death

It is now time to lighten the service with some words of comfort and to honour the memory of the deceased.

---- had a deep love for her family and countless friends, and the following words are a tribute to that enduring and unconditional love.

To be loved truly by someone is a rare thing.

A wife's love, a husband's love, a mother and father's love, a grandparent's love and a friend's love is something that is never lost.

It is a love that can't be described.

If love is one thing that can be passed down from generation to generation then, ----, you have done your job.

For the love that was in your heart is now in ours and we can never forget you.

Your love surrounds us every day.

You are part of us forever.

We love you, ----.

Rest in peace.

Barry H. Young

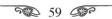

Don't think of her as gone away,
Her journey's just begun.
Life holds so many facets;
This earth is only one.

Just think of her as resting
From the sorrow and the tears
In a place of warmth and comfort,
Where there are no days and years.

Think how she must be wishing
That we could know today
How nothing but our sadness
Can really pass away.

And think of her as living
In the hearts of those she touched,
For nothing loved is ever lost,
And she was loved so much.

Author unknown

A man is a success who lived well,
Laughed often and gave much.

Who gained the respect of others and the love of children,
Who filled his destiny and accomplished his tasks.

Who left a treasure book of memories,
Who never lacked appreciation in others or failed to express it,
Who looked for the best in others and gave the best that he had.

Adapted from Bessie A. Stanley, 'What constitutes success'

We all know how much ---- loved life, and the following verse sums up
how ---- would want us to remember a life full of joy.

Do Not Stand at my Grave and Weep

Do not stand at my grave and weep
I am not there; I do not sleep.
I am a thousand winds that blow,
I am the diamond glints on snow,
I am the sun on ripened grain,
I am the gentle autumn rain.
When you awaken in the morning's hush
I am the swift uplifting rush
Of quiet birds in circling flight.
I am the soft starlight at night.
Do not stand at my grave and cry,
I am not there; I did not die.

Author unknown (attributed to Mary Frye)

These words can be said and appreciated by the family of the deceased if there was evidence of overwhelming love by a married couple.

---- and ---- shared a wonderful marriage and togetherness, and these
few words are a tribute to that wonderful happening.

If two are caring, as they're sharing life's hopes and fears,
If the music of laughter outweighs sadness of tears,
Then marriage is togetherness.

If both derive pleasure from mere presence of each other,
Yet when parted no jealousies restrict, worry or smother,
Then marriage is freedom.

If achievements mean more when they benefit two,
And consideration is shown with each point of view,
Then marriage is respect.

And if togetherness, freedom and respect are combined,
With a joy that words can never fully define,
Then marriage is love.

Author unknown

Once you have opened proceedings, it is time to move on to the heart of the service.

These beautiful words perfectly represent the life of ----.

> *Life is an opportunity, benefit from it.*
> *Life is beauty, admire it.*
> *Life is bliss, taste it.*
> *Life is a dream, realise it.*
> *Life is a challenge, meet it.*
> *Life is a duty, complete it.*
> *Life is a game, play it.*
> *Life is a promise, fulfil it.*
> *Life is sorrow, overcome it.*
> *Life is a song, sing it.*
> *Life is a struggle, accept it.*
> *Life is a tragedy, confront it.*
> *Life is an adventure, dare it.*
> *Life is luck, make it.*
> *Life is too precious, do not destroy it.*
> *Life is life, fight for it.*

Mother Teresa

4 Readings, eulogies and tributes: the heart of the service

The role of the celebrant in the heart of a good service is to ensure that the bereaved are provided with appropriate readings and verses, and encouraged to pay tribute in their own words. It is also important to ensure that their wishes and abilities are respected.

In many cases, a family member or friend will present a tribute or reading, but the celebrant will be left to present the actual eulogy. At other times, a good friend or relative will present the eulogy in whole. It may be that you are asked to take care of all the readings, or at least prepare the readings for the bereaved to read. These options should be discussed with the family at the initial interview (see Chapter 2).

In this chapter we will look at how you can go about preparing the heart of the service, including readings you can recommend to the family if they are not sure what they would like. I have also included the important and delicate topic of religion's role in a celebrant's service. Of course, if a funeral celebrant has been asked to handle a service rather than a traditional church ceremony, then it would seem the bereaved are not adhering to any specific church or religion. However, that does not preclude us from integrating meaningful parts of a religious service into our own ceremonies.

Eulogies

Preparing your eulogy

A good celebrant should always prepare a eulogy as though there will be no other speakers at the ceremony. Regardless of whether there are several friends or relatives giving eulogies, it is wise to be prepared in case they falter. It is always possible that the grief of the occasion will get the better of the person giving the eulogy, who will often have a close relationship with the deceased. In such cases, important information may not be conveyed or summed up as clearly as the bereaved may wish.

Having your own eulogy prepared also allows you to sum up at the conclusion by adding something extra, widening the perspective of the tribute being paid to the deceased. The eulogy may not have included something that you recorded during the interview—something light-hearted, something important or even something trivial. The people giving the tributes or eulogies may not have been at the initial interview with the bereaved, and therefore may not have the information that you have collected.

Preparing a eulogy for someone you may not have met may seem a mighty responsibility—and in some ways it is—but I often find that there is plenty of material from the interviews to use, and it's just a matter of getting started.

Introducing the eulogy

Rather than aim for anything grandiose, something like the following simple introduction can start the ball rolling:

> *In the next few minutes it is my privilege to share with you the life of ---- ----. As well as sharing in his life, we also share in our grief for his passing. And after speaking with the family, I know they would not want you to grieve in hurt or pain but grieve in the joy that ---- has given, has received and has shared with each of you.*

See Chapters 6–10 for sample eulogies used in different types of funeral services.

Introducing eulogies by family and friends

If it has been decided at the interview that family and friends will prepare readings and tributes, you will simply invite the nominated speakers to come forward to deliver their personal tributes to the deceased. For example:

> *As a tribute to Arthur, his daughter, Maria, will now share her thoughts with us. Please come forward, Maria.*

Of course, it's your duty to carefully record the names of all speakers and participants in the service so that you can announce them at the correct times in the service.

Remember, too, to request that those speaking bring a written copy of their eulogy to the service. That way, if they do find themselves unable to go on, another friend or family member—or you, as the celebrant—can continue on with the words the speaker has chosen.

Tributes and readings

As I mentioned in Chapter 2, I always carry inspirational readings with me to my initial interviews with the bereaved. If family members or friends do not wish to speak or are not sure which readings to choose, I then offer them something from my selection. Some of these are reproduced below.

During the service, the reading can be broken up into the required number of segments and presented accordingly. I have witnessed many wonderful moments of this happening—of different speakers delivering different parts of a reading, or of people (especially children) speaking in tandem. Remember, though, that you will have much more experience with funerals than many of the bereaved, so be the initiator.

Sample readings

The following are some very meaningful examples of readings.

A tribute to a father and grandfather

A wonderful husband, father, brother,
And friend so loving and kind,
What beautiful memories you leave behind.

Sharing and caring and always content,
Loved and respected wherever you went.

A happy smile, a heart of gold:
You were the best this world could hold.

A special husband, father, brother
And grandfather so kind and true:
What beautiful memories we all have of you.

Author unknown

A tribute to a mother's love

A beautiful poem for mothers is Helen Steiner Rice's 'A Mother's Love'. You can find this poem on various internet sites.

Here are two more tributes to mothers:

A mother is a wonderful creature constructed almost entirely of love. And this she can express in a million ways. From hugs and kisses and good cooking, and patient listening, to stern lectures, strict rules, and repeated uses of the word 'No'.

Like snowflakes, no two mothers are alike, but they have a number of things in common. Name anything … a mother can be found washing it, polishing it, getting rid of it, repairing it, packing it, teaching it, redecorating it, loving it or talking it over.

A mother cares for almost anything. Gardens, pets, the state of the nation, the worn spot on the rug, hungry people and, most of all, her husband and her children. For these she will do anything, and fight for anything necessary to their happiness.

A mother is not always an angel. She will often disagree with you, expect too much of you, question your choice of friends and bring up the subject of work when you feel the least energetic. But she's always ready to help when you need her.

You don't always tell a mother how much you love her, or how much you hope the most wonderful things in the world will come to her, because there are no words that express feelings so deep and sincere. Somehow, though, you feel she understands what's in your heart. Mothers always do.

Author unknown

Mum, we want you to know that we loved you.
You were a very important part of our lives.

Our relationship, our memories and moments shared,
And the love you've given us,
Are all so very precious to us.

We count our blessings to have had a mother like you,
And we hope you realised
That you have always been our inspiration.

You have guided us in each decision,
And encouraged us to reach for every dream.

You have helped us through your guidance, your wisdom
And the strength of your love,
To become the people you wanted us to be.

We want you to know
That though we may not have told you often enough,
You mean so much more to us than words can say.
We thank you and we love you with all our hearts.

Author unknown

A tribute to a grandparent

For those times that we needed you most,
For all those lovely things you have done for us.

For being a truly wonderful Grandma
For all the things and a million more,
Which seem to us a daily chore,
We give our thanks and all our love.

We miss you so much, our wonderful Grandma,
You showed us how to cope in life,
Your example was your will.

You showed us courage and compassion,
You were the one that was always there.
You were the one that always cared.

We will never forget your quiet strength.
You did so much for all of us.
You are impossible to replace.

You truly were the family key,
You were the force behind us all.

You were the greatest Grandma we've ever met.

Author unknown

A partner's tribute

The following poem is an example of one a loving partner might read for a partner they have lost. .

My love, you gave yourself to me
And life caught fire from your spark.
But then, like sunshine, here and gone
You left us in the mournful dark.

The time we shared was full of warmth
Our flame sustained us through the years
And now it lights the path ahead
Between the silence and the tears.

Your memory will not fade away
To muted tones of black and white.
How could such blazing colour leave
The earth without a dazzling flight?

So hear this now, my love, my life
Since your sweet sunshine left the blue
A brilliant rainbow's spanned the sky—
And that is how we'll think of you.

Anon

Here is another example of a poem read by a bereaved partner.

A man I love is missing,
A voice I love is still.
A place is vacant to my heart
That no one else can fill.

No matter how my life may change
Or whatever I may do,
I will always cherish the memories,
Of the years I spent with you,
Forever in my heart.

Author unknown

Tributes to provide comfort

One tribute which mourners find very comforting is a poem called 'Remember Me' by David Harkins. It was read out at the Queen Mother's funeral in 2002, and you can find the poem on many internet sites.

Here are some more special words of comfort for loved ones.

Cry Not for Me

I have lived so well upon this earth
I have followed many paths to reach the sun
If I had troubles, or pain, or heartaches
I cherished more the smiles, a thousand more, when one
Had said to me in friendship—'I wish you well!'
They were sweet words I treasured long.
To the hilltops, to the clouds to the moon and stars beyond
To a pasture glistening with fresh rain.
To the sea with white tipped waves—I run
So, cry not for me, my friends, hear the music in my heart
And kiss my memory 'Farewell'.

Ruth Van Gramberg (extract)

A universal tribute

Though I depart this way,
A life not able to complete,
Your everlasting love will shine.
Every moment in every day.

Thoughts and memories, so few in time,
Special in every way
Will always travel in my mind,
Of a very special day.

My love will always be with you,
As yours remains with me.
For this alone will see me through,
Until we meet another day.

Author unknown

A tribute to an inspiring person

All people inspire us in some way, but the following is an example of what you might say about a person who had a particularly significant impact on the lives of others, and who you feel had a 'message' for those who are grieving. An appropriate time would be during your eulogy, or at its conclusion.

I can't help feeling that there is something special about today. You see, you are the positive evidence that ---- influence hasn't just ceased because he has left us.

In some special way he has even more strength now to bring people together, to touch something down deep in us. You can't help feeling that there's something special ---- wants to say to us—something different to each one of us, according to our strengths and our uniqueness.

For some, it may be not to put off what you want to do in life. For some, to give more of ourselves to others like he did. For some, not to take life too seriously, because you never know how brief it might be. For others, to take life more seriously because it is so fragile.

We all may need to reassess our values and priorities and recognise how trivial the things are that divide us. Or we may all realise that we should attend to the little things, which are really the big things—like telling people how much they mean to us, how much we appreciate them, even how much we love them—before it is too late.

He might even be challenging us to make our own lives more meaningful and worthwhile. And if we can do this, what we are really doing for ---- is giving continuing purpose to his life, some meaning to his passing, and a living and lasting continuing stake in our lives. We are making sure he is not just part of the past in our memories or of the present in our grief, but is very much part of our future lives.

And then, someday looking back, we will see ---- memory, not as it is today—a tear-filled cloud—but as a beautiful light on our horizon, giving our lives an extra richness and dimension of meaning.

Religious readings and prayers

Even though the funeral services you conduct may not adhere to a specific religious tradition, the family or friends of the deceased may request some religious input into the service. If so, it's important that this can be provided. Our very flexibility as civil celebrants allows us to include religious aspects in the service if family members ask for it.

Religion plays an important role in many people's lives and religious ceremonies and rituals are traditionally part of marking many of life's most important milestones. So even when a civil celebrant is asked to perform a funeral service, free from the doctrines and ceremonies of any specific religion, it will often be appropriate to include religious readings and prayers. This is especially so if some of the bereaved are members of a specific church.

Sample readings

Footprints in the Sand

One night I had a dream. I dreamed I was walking along a beach with the Lord. Across the sky flashed scenes from my life. For each scene I noticed two sets of footprints in the sand, one belonging to me and the other to the Lord. When the last scene of my life flashed before me, I looked back at the footprints in the sand.

I noticed that many times along the path of my life there was only one set of footprints. I also noticed that it happened at the very lowest and saddest times in my life.

This really bothered me and I questioned the Lord about it.

'Lord, you said that once If decided to follow you, you would walk with me all the way. But I have noticed that during the most troublesome times in my life there is only one set of footprints.

I don't understand why, when I needed you most, you should leave me.'

The Lord replied, 'My precious, precious child, I love you and I would never, never leave you during your times of trial, tribulation and suffering.

When you saw only one set of footprints, it was then I carried you.'

Author unknown

Abou Ben Adhem

Abou Ben Adhem (may his tribe increase!)
Awoke one night from a deep dream of peace,
And saw, within the moonlight in his room,
Making it rich, and like a lily in bloom,
An Angel writing in a book of gold.

Exceeding peace had made Ben Adhem bold,
And to the Presence in the room he said,
'What writest thou?'—The vision raised its head,
And with a look made of all sweet accord,
Answered, 'The names of those who love the Lord.'

'And is mine one?' said Abou. 'Nay, not so',
Replied the Angel. Abou spoke more low,
But cheerily still, and said, 'I pray thee then,
write me as one who loves his fellow man.'

The Angel wrote and vanished. The next night
It came again with a great wakening light,
And showed the names whom love of God had bless'd,
And lo! Ben Adhem's name led all the rest.

James Henry Leigh Hunt

A loving wife handed me these words to read on her behalf to her husband.

We are just a number in life's big record book.
So there's no point in being scared
When it's our turn to look inside
The gates of heaven, to see the great unknown
And meet with all our loved ones,
And never be alone.

Believing in the after-life
Will help you through the day,
For one thing's very certain:
Death will not go away.

But know that Heaven's waiting,
Your reward for work well done,
Look forward to the other side
Your new life's just begun.

Author unknown

Scripture readings

John 14:1–6 (adapted)

Jesus promised his followers a place in his Father's house.

He said to them, 'Let not your heart be troubled; believe in God,
believe also in me. In my Father's house are many rooms; if it were
not so, would I have told you that I go to prepare a place for you? And
when I go and prepare a place for you, I will come again and take you
to myself, that where I am you may be also. And you know the way
where I am going.'

Thomas said to him, 'Lord, we do not know where you are going; how can we know the way?'

Jesus said to him, 'I am the way, and the truth, and the life; no one comes to the Father, but by me.'

The 23rd Psalm

The Lord is my shepherd: I shall not want.
He maketh me to lie down in green pastures:
He leadeth me beside the still waters.
He restoreth my soul:

He leadeth me in the paths of righteousness
For his name's sake.
Yea though I walk through the valley of the shadow of death
I will fear no evil:
For thou art with me the rod and thy staff they comfort me.
Thou preparest a table before me
In the presence of mine enemies:
Thou anointest my head with oil:
My cup runneth over.

Surely goodness and mercy shall follow me
All the days of my life:
And I will dwell in the house of the Lord forever.

1 Corinthians 13:4–8 (adapted)

Love is patient, love is kind. It does not envy, it does not boast, it is not proud. It is not rude, it is not self-seeking, it is not easily angered, it keeps no record of wrongs. Love does not delight in evil but rejoices with the truth. It always protects, always trusts, always hopes, always perseveres. Love never fails.

Ecclesiastes 3:1–8 (adapted)

To everything there is a season,
And a time for every purpose.

A time to be born and a time to die,
A time to weep and a time to laugh,
A time to mourn and a time to dance.

A time to get and a time to lose,
A time to keep and a time to give away.

A time of war and a time of peace,
A time to be happy and a time to love.

And most of all a time of contentment.

Other meaningful Bible readings

- Psalm 46:1–3 ('God is our refuge and strength …')

- Psalm 25: 1–11 ('To you, O Lord, I lift up my soul …')

- Isaiah 54:10 ('For the mountains may depart …')

- Matthew 11:28–30 ('Come to me, all who labour …')

- Mark 10:13–16 ('And they were bringing children to him …')

- John 3:16 ('For God so loved the world …')

- John 5:19–29 ('… For whatever the Father does, that the Son does likewise …')

- John 6:35–40 ('Jesus said to them, "I am the bread of life …"')

- John 11:17–27 ('Now when Jesus came, he found that Lazarus …')

- John 11:25 ('… I am the resurrection and the life …')

- Romans 8:31–39 ('… If God is with us, who can be against us? …')

- 2 Corinthians 13–14 ('This is the third time I am coming to you …')

- Philippians 3:8–21 ('…For his sake I have suffered the loss of all things …')

- Revelation 21:1–7 ('Then I saw a new heaven and a new earth …')

Religious prayers

Here is a suitable prayer that can be used on almost any occasion.

Eternal Father, God of all consolation,
In your unending love and mercy for us,
You turn the darkness of death into the dawn of new life.

Be our refuge and strength in sorrow.
We ask that you take ---- into your fold.

For as your son, our Lord Jesus Christ,
By dying for us conquered death.
And by rising restored us to life,

So may we go forward in faith to meet him,
And after our life on earth.
We ask this through Jesus Christ our Lord.

Amen.

The Prayer of St Francis

Lord, make me an instrument of your peace.
Where there is hatred, let me sow love;
Where there is injury, pardon;
Where there is discord, unity;
Where there is doubt, faith;
Where there is error, truth;
Where there is despair, hope;
Where there is sadness, joy;
Where there is darkness, light.

O Divine Master,
Grant that I may not so much seek to be consoled as to console;
To be understood, as to understand;
To be loved, as to love;
For it is in giving that we receive,
It is in pardoning that we are pardoned,
And it is in dying that we are born to Eternal Life.

Amen.

A good introduction to 'The Lord's Prayer' is: 'For those of you who wish, please join me in saying "The Lord's Prayer"'.

The Lord's Prayer

Our Father, which art in heaven.
Hallowed be thy name.
Thy Kingdom come.
Thy will be done, on Earth
As it is in heaven.
Give us this day our daily bread.
And forgive us our trespasses
As we forgive those who trespass against us.
And lead us not into temptation
But deliver us from evil.
For thine is the Kingdom,
The power and the glory,
For ever and ever.

Amen.

A Prayer for the One Who is Left

Lord, the trouble about life just now
Is that I seem to have all things
Which don't matter, and to have
Lost all the things that do matter.

I have life;
I have enough money to live on:
I have plenty to occupy me:
But I am alone
And sometimes I feel that
Nothing can make up for that.

Lord, compel me to see
The meaning of my faith.
Make me to realise
That I have hope
As well as a memory, and
The unseen cloud of witness
Is around me;
That you meant it when
You said that you would
Always be with me;
And make me to realise that
As long as you leave me here
There is something that
I am meant to do;
And in doing it, help me
To find the comfort and the courage
That I need to go on.

Amen.

Author unknown

The Irish Blessing

May the road rise to meet you
May the wind be always at your back
May the sun shine upon your face,
The rains fall softly upon the fields
And, until we meet again, may you be held
In the palm of God's hand.

Summing up afterwards

Even if the bereaved have taken the opportunity to perform a great number of readings and eulogies celebrating their lost loved one, after the speakers have completed their tributes, thank them all and then sum up.

If the service is held in a chapel, with the committal taking place at the cemetery or crematorium, the following words are appropriate:

> *That concludes this part of the service here at the Penrose Chapel. The cortege will now leave for the Northcote Cemetery where the committal will take place.*

Be sure to find out when refreshments are taking place, however; they may be taking place before the committal, rather than afterwards.

The next step in the funeral service is the committal. This is the final and most emotional stage of a ceremony, and we will look at it in the next chapter.

5 *The committal*

The committal is the extremely heart-wrenching part of a funeral service where the deceased is committed to the ground in a casket, or interred. It is a very solemn and difficult time for the family and friends of the deceased person, so you should ensure your words are sensitive and carefully chosen. As we touched on in Chapter 1, at a burial or committal you should speak for no longer than five to eight minutes.

In this chapter we will look at some readings you might use prior to the committal and during the committal.

Readings prior to committal

Many celebrants go straight into the committal after the readings and eulogies have been completed. As this is a very painful part of the service for grieving loved ones, I often try to soften the event by introducing it with some meaningful words.

To introduce a reading before the committal, you might say something like the following (depending on the reading):

> *Here is a very special reading, and to feel its sacred meaning I ask you to become as one with ----.*

or:

> *Here are some lovely and meaningful words that I say to ---- on behalf of you, her family and her friends.*

or:

> *When someone we love dies, we are faced with trying to understand one of life's great mysteries. But I believe the following words are a way of looking at death that is comforting, and that makes it just a little easier to understand.*

One particularly moving piece to read prior to a committal is 'The Dash' by Linda Ellis. Below are some other suggestions for readings you could use.

To One in Sorrow

Let me come in where you are weeping, friend,
And let me take your hand.
I, who have known a sorrow such as yours,
Can understand.
Let me come in—I would be very still
Beside you in your grief;
I would not bid you cease your weeping, friend,
Tears bring relief.
Let me come in—and hold your hand,
For I have known a sorrow such as yours,
And understand.

Grace Noll Crowell

When I Am Gone

When I am gone, fear not to say my name
Nor speak of me in hushed tones
As though it were a shame for me to die.
Let me figure in your daily life,
Speak of my loves and hates;
And how I used to talk and laugh.
This way I'll be forever in your memory.

Remember the good times:
Remember the laughter, not the tears
The loving, not the anger
The courage, not the pain.
My generous heart is still at last
And I do not want anyone to be sad.

Author unknown

Imagine

If you love me
Then know that our love is eternal,
That the bond we share together
Will go on forever.

Imagine that I am staying with you
For a while in time.
Imagine that it is the end of my day,
And I leave you to go into the next room.
Imagine that the room I've entered
Is filled with joy and peace and love,
Of old friends who are delighted to see me,
Of beautiful flowers, of healing warmth,
And magic rainbow colours.

Imagine how happy I will be
In that magnificent room.

One day you will come into my room
And see me more beautiful, and happier
Than you have ever seen me before.
You will feel the same peace and joy
That I am feeling.

If you can imagine this,
Then you will understand
That death is not an ending
But merely a passing from one room to another
In the mansions of time.

Life goes on forever
And love will never end.

Yvonne Goddard

I had a dream, I dreamt I left you,
I went to a beautiful place,
Where day was night, and night was day,
Where there were no hours, no minutes,
For time stood still.

And all around were beautiful flowers,
Healing warmth and magic rainbow colours.
With beauty around me,
A winding path reached out before me.

And there beckoning me were my loved ones,
Those sacred friends who had gone before me.
We embraced, kissed, sang and rejoiced.

My eyes were strangely dry.
I was to learn that this place sheds no tears.
And then I thought of you—your hurt,
Your sorrow today so sad for me.

So I ask of you, tomorrow smile for me.
Think of me with gladness.
For my strength is your strength,
My peace is your peace.
I have never left you,
And you will never leave me.

Until we meet again then,
But not before you're ready,
I'll be waiting for you.

Look for me on a winding path that has no end.

Barry H. Young

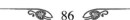

You gave us your love and a reason to live.
You've been our best friend for so many years.

We've shared happy times and also our tears.
There's no one that means as much as you do.

After all you've done for us,
And all we've been through together.

So we'll never be parted—it just cannot be.

For you know we love you,
And we know you love us.

For as long as we can dream
For as long as we can think
As long as we have memory
We will think of you, ----.

For as long as we have eyes to see,
And ears to hear, and lips to speak,
We will speak of you, ----.

As long as we have a heart to feel
A soul stirring within us,
An imagination to hold you,
We will remember you, ----.

As long as there is time
As long as there is love
As long as we have the breath to speak your name
We will love you, ----.

Author unknown

One at Rest

Think of me as one at rest,
For me you should not weep
I have no pain no troubled thoughts
For I am just asleep.
The living thinking me that was,
Is now forever still
And life goes on without me now,
As time forever will.

If your heart is heavy now
Because I've gone away
Dwell not long upon it, friend
For none of us can stay.
Those of you who liked me,
I sincerely thank you all
And those of you who loved me,
I thank you most of all.

And in my fleeting lifespan,
As time went rushing by
I found some time to hesitate,
To laugh, to love, to cry.
Matters it now if time began,
If time will ever cease?
I was here, I used it all,
And now I am at peace.

Author unknown

One I like to use as an alternative to 'One at Rest' is the following, an extract of a poem by Henry Scott Holland, a professor of divinity at Oxford University in the early 1900s.

Death is Nothing at All

Death is nothing at all. It does not count.
I have only slipped away into the next room.

Whatever we were to each other, that we are still.
Call me by the old familiar name.

Speak of me in the easy way which you always used.
Put no difference into your tone.

Wear no forced air of solemnity or sorrow.
Laugh as we always laughed at the little jokes
That we enjoyed together.

Play, smile, think of me, pray for me.
Let my name be ever the household word
That it always was.

Let it be spoken without an effort,
Without the ghost of a shadow upon it.

Life means all that it ever meant.
It is the same as it ever was.

There is absolute and unbroken continuity.

Why should I be out of mind
Because I am out of sight?

I am but waiting for you,
For an interval,
Somewhere very near,
Just round the corner.

All is well.

Henry Scott Holland

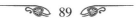

Here's another much-used reading, but one that's always meaningful when used appropriately. It can be used at any part of a service.

For each of us here today life is a journey.
It is a journey in time.

Our birth is the beginning of that journey
And it is important to believe
That death is not the end but the destination.

For our life is a journey that takes us
From youth to age
From innocence to awareness,
From ignorance to knowledge,
From foolishness to wisdom,
From weakness to strength and often back again.

It takes us from offence to forgiveness,
From loneliness to friendship,
From pain to compassion,
From fear to faith.

From defeat to defeat to defeat,
Until looking backwards or ahead
We see that victory does not lie
At some high point along the way

But in having made the journey,
Step by step.

Author unknown

Her Role Down Here is Done

Her loving soul has touched us all,
She didn't need to stay:
Her spirit touched each one of us
Before it sailed away.

We all know souls arrive on earth
With special roles to fill,
And hers has fully played its part,
Her memory guides us still.

She had a very special soul
She stayed but just a while:
So if, or when, you're feeling sad
Recall her with a smile.

For then you'll know inside your heart
The reasons why she's gone:
And never feel too empty that
Her role down here is done.

Her spirit touched each one of us,
No other ever could.
Forever we will cherish her
The way we know we should.

Author unknown

Life does proceed, when a loved one leaves.
But it's difficult for us who are left to grieve.

We'll pick ourselves up and try again.
We'll make the effort to function again.

It won't be easy, as we well know.
But we won't give up—the change made us grow.

We loved ---- so much, and fate was unkind.
She went away first—she left us behind.

The pain in our hearts will remain yet awhile.
But yesterday's gone. Tomorrow we'll try to smile.

Author unknown

The tide recedes but leaves behind,
Bright seashells on the sand.

The sun goes down but gentle warmth,
Still lingers on the land.

The music stops and yet,
It echoes on in sweet refrain.

For every joy that passes,
Something beautiful remains.

Author unknown

A tribute to a lost partner

The following is special reading from a husband to his beloved wife or a wife to her beloved husband.

You Will Always Be There

The rays of light filtered through the sentinels of
trees this morning.
I sat in the garden and contemplated.

The serenity and beauty of my feelings and
surroundings completely captivated me …
I thought of you.

I discovered you tucked away in the shadows
of the trees.
Then rediscovered you, on the smiles of the flowers
As the sun penetrated the petals …
In the rhythm of the leaves falling in the garden ...
In the freedom of the birds as they fly
Searching as you do ...

I'm very happy to have found you ...
Now you will never leave me for I will always find you
In the beauty of life.

Author unknown

A Song of Living

Because I have loved life, I shall have no sorrow to die.
I have sent up my gladness on wings, to be lost in the blue of the sky.
I have run and leaped with the rain, I have taken the wind to my breast.
My cheek like a drowsy child to the face of the earth I have pressed.
Because I have loved life, I shall have no sorrow to die.

I have kissed young Love on the lips, I have heard his song to the end.
I have struck my hand like a seal in the loyal hand of a friend.
I have known the peace of heaven, the comfort of work done well.
I have longed for death in the darkness and risen alive out of hell.
Because I have loved life, I shall have no sorrow to die.

I give a share of my soul to the world where my course is run.
I know that another shall finish the task I must leave undone.
I know that no flower, no flint was in vain on the path I trod.
As one looks on a face through a window, through life I have looked
*   on God.*
Because I have loved life, I shall have no sorrow to die.

Amelia Josephine Burr

I have got to leave you.
Bid me farewell, my family and my friends.

I bow to you all and take my departure,
Here I give back the keys to the door.

I give up all claims to my house,
I ask only kind words from you.

We were neighbours, family and friends for so long,
But I have received more than I could give.

Now the day has dawned,
And the lamp that lit my dark corner is out.

A summons has come,
And I am ready for the journey.

Author unknown

You closed your eyes and were taken to a beautiful place,
And left us to try to understand.

Others are taken, this we know,
But you were ours and we loved you so.

You'll be in our thoughts every day,
In our hearts you will always stay.

A silent prayer and a tear, too,
We will always love you and miss you.

Go with our love. In time we'll understand.
Go with our blessing, into loving, caring hands.

Author unknown

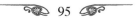

The following is a very poignant committal farewell and should only be used at times when it will not appear too insensitive to advise mourners to move beyond their grief and let their lost loved ones go.

Miss me — but let me go

When I come to the end of the road,
And the sun has set for me,
I want no rites in a gloom-filled room;
Why cry for a soul set free?

Miss me a little — but not too long
and not with your head bowed low,
Remember the love that we once shared.
Miss me — but let me go.

For this is a journey we all must take,
And each must go alone.
It's all part of the master plan,
A step on the road to home.

When you are lonely and sick of heart,
Go to the friends we know.
Bury your sorrows in doing good deeds.
Miss me — but let me go.

Author unknown

The committal process

The actual committal process should be formal and brief as this is the most heart-wrenching stage of the ceremony.

The funeral director will play soft appropriate music. Some funeral directors prefer not to have music as they think it takes away the solemnity of the moment when the coffin/casket disappears from view. Others think it takes away the deep sorrow and harshness of the moment and makes it more bearable.

Examples of committals

Non-religious committals

Please be upstanding.

Tenderly and reverently we commit ----'s body to be cremated.

We are grateful for the life that has been lived, and for all that life has meant to us. We are glad ---- lived.

We are glad we saw his face and felt the pressure of his hand. We cherish the memories of his words, his deeds and his character.

We cherish his friendship. And most of all we cherish his love.

Today we have acknowledged our appreciation for the privilege of sharing a part of ----'s life.

Even though her death has meant a physical break in the links of the chain that binds you to each other, the influence and effect of ----'s life is still evident now as we speak her name.

And so we say that we are glad ---- lived. We are glad we saw her face. We are glad we felt her touch and heard her laughter.

We are comforted to know that her pain has ended, her spirit is free and that she leaves this life satisfied in the knowledge that she has accomplished her tasks.

We will forever cherish the memory of ----'s love, her resilience, her wisdom, her friendship, and most of all her love.

Committals with a religious theme

It is now time to say goodbye to ----. There is sadness in his passing but we take comfort in the hope that one day we shall see him again. Although this congregation will disperse in sorrow, the mercy of God will gather us together again into the joy of his kingdom.

Please be upstanding.

May eternal rest be granted unto ----, O Lord, and let perpetual light shine upon him.

Tenderly and reverently, we will commit the body of ----- to the purifying elements, grateful for the life that has been lived and for all that his life has meant to us.

We now leave ---- in peace. With much love and respect we bid him farewell. Thus in thinking of ----, let us leave this place in quietness of spirit and live with concern and affection for one another.

Please be upstanding.

Let us commend ---- into the hands of God, our Maker and Redeemer. O God our heavenly Father, who by thy mighty power has given us life, and by thy loving kindness has bestowed upon us new life in Jesus Christ.

We commend to thy merciful keeping thy servant ----, our loved one here departed.

Take ---- into the love and safety of your everlasting comfort.

Through Jesus Christ thy son of God

Who died and rose again to save us.

Amen.

Closing words

After the committal, it is appropriate to ask the mourners to be seated as a final musical tribute is played. This will usually be a song the family or friends have chosen.

To conclude the service, it's important to find some closing words that will soothe the mourners, bringing some peace and hope to all.

Prior to the benediction the following words can form an inspirational and meaningful conclusion to the service. Once again, though, be sure to review each situation and only use where appropriate for the circumstances of the person's passing.

These are some final words I say to you from ----.

> *Now I am gone, release me, let me go.*
> *You have so many things to see and do.*
> *You musn't tie yourself to me with grief.*
>
> *Be happy that we had some wonderful years.*
> *I love you, my loved ones, and you can only guess*
> *How much you gave to me of happiness.*
>
> *I thank you for the love and the joy*
> *And understanding you all have shown me.*
> *But now it's time I travelled alone.*
>
> *So grieve awhile for me, if grieve you must,*
> *Then let your grief be comforted by trust.*
> *It's only for a while that we must part.*
> *So bless those memories that lie within your heart*
> *That mean so much to me,*
> *And release me, let me go.*

Author unknown

Benediction

Most celebrants do not conclude the service with a religious benediction. The one I have written is not a religious benediction and accordingly gives quality, meaning and finality to the service.

We now leave the memory of our beloved ---- in peace. With enduring love and respect we bid her farewell.

May you find richness and example in your memories of ----. May you find strength and support in your love for one another and may you find peace in your hearts.

If there are many young people in the congregation who had an affinity with the deceased, the following words can be included in the benediction after the second sentence.

And let us promise her to have a devotion to things worthwhile and make our living of real and meaningful worth.

Now we come to the end of Part 2, having explored a range of readings that may be used in funeral services. Of course there are many more you might use and adapt for your own services; the internet offers a range of readings on many websites, as do some published books, including those on the 'Recommended reading' list at the back of this book. We move now into some sample services for different occasions, using a selection of the readings we have just seen. The aim is to give you some idea of the flow of a service, and to suggest appropriate readings for the different kinds of funeral services you may be asked to conduct.

PART
3

Sample Services

6 *An elderly lady*

The following section of this book aims to help you write a special service applicable to particular occasions. Each chapter will contain a choice of readings from earlier chapters.

If you are in the process of completing your studies to become a funeral celebrant, or have already completed them, you will find my structure different from what you have been taught. Stay with the structure you have learned if you are comfortable with it, but it may help you to be aware of alternatives. The sample services here have worked overwhelmingly well for me, and you may find parts of them helpful to you, too.

Starting the service

You might start a service for an elderly lady by playing appropriate music—either the choice of the bereaved or the funeral director. You could play it for 10 minutes prior to the start of the service.

An opening reading

> *They say it's a beautiful journey*
> *From the old world to the new.*
> *Someday we'll all take that journey,*
> *Up the stairway that leads to you.*
>
> *And when we reach that garden*
> *Where all are free from pain,*
> *We'll put our arms around you, ----,*
> *And we'll never part again.*

For God looked around his garden,
And found an empty space,
Then He looked upon the Earth,
And found a lady full of grace.

A golden heart had stopped beating,
Two hands were laid to rest.
The garden must be beautiful,
Because He only takes the best.

Author unknown

Introduction

Today we are here to celebrate the life of a lovely, gracious lady who has been lost to us. And I ask that you feel free to be at one with your sorrow, your sadness and your memories, but also I ask you to feel the gladness, the happiness, the purpose and the serenity of a life so well lived. I speak of ---- ----.

At the conclusion of the service you are invited to the Cedar Room for refreshments, a chat and to recollect those special times you spent with ----. Her passing has left a deep sadness in our lives.

This time we spend together today is to remember ---- and to allow our sorrow and sadness to surface and be expressed in words, in tears, in reflection or in whatever way is meaningful to each of us. We gather to remember---- and to say goodbye.

Our being together here is a support and comfort for each of us, whether members of the family or caring friends. Our collective sorrow and grief becomes a collective strength, enabling us to find closure and move on without the physical presence of our beloved ----. Let us remember ----'s life with gratitude, joy, gladness and love.

When we lose someone dear to us the hurt can be almost unbearable, yet somehow we seem to get through it. And I believe that it is because we feel such pain—because the inner ache is so great—that the grief and heartache we feel bears witness to the depths of our love. You see, grief is a great indicator and measure of love. It simply cannot and does not exist except where there has been love.

I thank you for your presence here today, united in strength and love to remember a life well-lived.

Amelia had a deep love for her family and countless friends, and the following words are a tribute to that enduring, unconditional love.

To be loved truly by someone is a rare thing.

A wife's love, a husband's love, a mother's love, a grandmother's love and a friend's love is something that is never lost.

It is a love that can't be described.

If love is one thing that can be passed down from generation to generation then, Amelia, you have done your job.

For the love that was in your heart is now in ours and we can never forget you.

*Your love surrounds us every day.
You are part of us forever.*

We love you, Amelia.

Rest in peace.

Barry H. Young

Words to soften grief

We grieve today with thoughts of Amelia foremost in our minds. Her passing has brought sorrow to her family and friends, particularly as the ties of love and friendship were so strong.

But while we think of Amelia passing with sadness and regret, we should recall her life with respect and happiness. You see, nothing can detract from the happiness and closeness you shared with Amelia. Nothing can affect the happiness and the joy of life that Amelia knew.

And nothing can change your love for her and her love for you. It can never be altered by time, circumstance or even by death. What has been—the past with all its meaning—is sacred and secure.

Be grateful that Amelia was part of your lives and let her influence—her character, her lovely warmth and her deeds—live on.

A grandchild's tribute

As a tribute to Amelia, her granddaughter, Karen, will now share her thoughts with us. Please come forward, Karen.

For those times that we needed you most,
For all those lovely things you have done for us.

For being a truly wonderful Nan,
For all the things and a million more,
Which seem to us a daily chore.

We give our thanks and all our love,
We miss you—so much, a wonderful Nan.

You showed us how to cope in life,
Your example was your will.

You showed us courage and compassion,
You were the one who was always there,
You were the one who always cared.

We will never forget your quiet strength.
You did so much for all of us.
You are impossible to replace.
You truly were the family key.
You were the force behind us all.
You were the greatest Nan we've ever met.

Author unknown

Thank you, ----, for those beautiful thoughts and images of ----.

Eulogy

In the next few minutes, it will be my privilege to share with you the life of Amelia Elizabeth Lethbridge.

Amelia was born in Perth on the 12th of May 1924. Her parents were Harold and Margaret. Amelia had a brother, Joseph, who she adored. They were very close and enjoyed their telephone calls to each other.

Amelia attended Thurston State School, as did her mother and brother. She then attended a business school, but combined this with studying something she truly loved—the piano. For three days each week she attended classes, completing a diploma in piano which qualified her to teach music.

Initially, business school led her into a position at the Gowers Foods factory and it was here she met James. He worked at Gowers as an engineer, and Amelia was employed as a secretary. They were married on the 21st of May 1944, in Perth, just after Amelia's twentieth birthday. Thus began a wonderful togetherness that was to take them through half a century of marriage.

Two beloved children, Adrian and Julie, blessed the marriage. When they themselves married, Amelia welcomed their partners Tanya and Paul warmly into the family, and they cherished her thoughtfulness and consideration. As time went on, Amelia's grandchildren, Ben and Karen, became her pride and joy.

Amelia had a most industrious business career. From Gowers Foods she moved to the Laguna Weaving Mills and was soon promoted within the company. In 1946 Amelia and James started their own ceramics manufacturing business, which was to become Amelia's lifetime pursuit of excellence. From humble beginnings, Amelia and James built their business from the ground up, extending their market range into tablewear and industrial design. In 1961 they sold the business and continued to work for the new owners.

Amelia and Tom moved southwards a little, to Kwinana, in 1975. Amelia continued her expertise in the manufacturing industry as an office manager for a local firm, and it was from that firm that Amelia retired.

Amelia had myriad interests. She played the piano beautifully, and in her youth was heard on radio and at many concerts and competitions. As a teenager Amelia was involved in many musical productions. Although she never worked as a music teacher, she lent her fine playing to many local theatre groups and musical societies over the years, as an accompanist and occasionally as musical director of local shows. She also passed on her musical talents to both her grandchildren, who each have continued the musical tradition of the family in their own ways.

Amelia's artistic bent was also evident in her beautiful paintings. In addition to her sewing, embroidery, crocheting and needlework, she enjoyed painting in watercolours. Many friends and family have examples of Amelia's work on their walls today. Her favourite colour was pink so there was always a rosy hue to be found in her lovely creations. Amelia also loved small and pretty things— so much so that she couldn't even bear to eat pretty chocolates she was given as gifts, or to use the lovely crockery she collected, but kept them for years.

Keeping abreast of current affairs was also important to Amelia. She did this by reading the daily newspapers and listening to the news. Walking into Amelia and James' house, one would always hear the sounds of Amelia's favourite ABC programs. Other countries also fascinated her, and Amelia and James' first trip overseas was in 1980, when they travelled to London, Paris and Spain with Adrian and Tanya. It was one of the highlights of her life. But Amelia and James were keen local travellers, too, researching and visiting many places around Australia that tourists often miss.

Amelia's warm and cheerful personality drew many people to her and she made countless friends. I refer to her school friends Beth and Gloria (both deceased); June and Lily from her Gowers days; Marjory, her lifelong friend from her young musical days; Arthur and Lorna, who shared her love of painting; and, of course her countless friends from here in Kwinana. One of those loyal friends was Meryl Partridge, so sadly lost to us earlier in the year.

Sadly, Amelia lived the last ten years without James, the love of her life. When he passed, she said she felt as if a door had shut or a window closed in her life. With stoical courage, though, she carried on, always looking on the bright side and setting a wonderful example to her family and friends. She continued to live an active and positive life from her home in Jasmine Road, her independence and strength of character shining through.

Amelia kept excellent health until, unfortunately, she was struck down by a debilitating heart condition. Within two years, she was admitted to hospital for the last time, and sadly it was there that she was lost to us, her loved ones by her side in a room full of love. The family would like me to thank the staff of St Catherine's Hospital, particularly the cardiac care staff, for their loving care and devotion to Amelia.

Amelia was a woman who added value and breathed life, love and example in everything she did. She loved a challenge, always being led on by what was over the next hill and what was around the next bend. Her life was characterised by strength, dignity, courage and achievement, and she truly made a difference to the lives of many. Although her last weeks were fraught with difficulties, her bravery, courage and spirit were unfailing.

All who were privileged to have known her—family, friends and colleagues alike—found that she gave life strength, substance and spirit to everyone around her. Her legacy of kindness, love and commitment will live on in our hearts and memories forever.

Readings and tributes

The Lord's Prayer

For those of you who wish to, please join me in saying 'The Lord's Prayer'.

Our Father, which art in heaven.
Hallowed be thy name.
Thy Kingdom come.
Thy will be done, on Earth
As it is in heaven.
Give us this day our daily bread.
And forgive us our trespasses
As we forgive those who trespass against us.
And lead us not into temptation
But deliver us from evil.
For thine is the Kingdom,
The power and the glory,
For ever and ever.

Amen.

Music

As a tribute to Amelia, we will now play the beautiful song 'Bridge Over Troubled Waters' sung by Russell Watson, one of Amelia's particular favourites. While this is playing, you may like to turn the pages of your memory like a book, and remember the special times you spent with Amelia.

Readings

I'd now like to say some lovely and meaningful words to Amelia, on behalf of you, her family and her friends.

You gave us your love and a reason to live.
You've been our best friend for so many years.

We've shared happy times and also our tears.
There's no one that means as much as you do.

After all you've done for us,
And all we've been through together.

So we'll never be parted—it just cannot be.

For you know we love you,
And we know you love us.

For as long as we can dream
For as long as we can think
As long as we have memory
We will think of you, Amelia.

For as long as we have eyes to see,
And ears to hear, and lips to speak,
We will speak of you, Amelia.

As long as we have a heart to feel
A soul stirring within us,
An imagination to hold you,
We will remember you, Amelia.

As long as there is time
As long as there is love
As long as we have the breath to speak your name
We will love you, Amelia.

Author unknown

The next reading is one you may find comforting, and may make death a little easier to understand. And to feel the real meaning I would ask that you, in your minds, become as one with Amelia.

Imagine

If you love me then know that our love is eternal,
That the bond we share together will go on forever.

Now imagine that I am staying with you
For a while in time.
Imagine that it is the end of my day,
And I leave you to go into the next room.

Imagine that the room that I have entered
Is filled with joy and peace and love.
Of loved ones and old friends who have gone before,
Who are delighted to see me.
Of beautiful flowers, of healing warmth
And magic rainbow colours.

Now imagine how happy I will be
In that magnificent room.
Now one day you will come into that magnificent room.
But not before you're ready.

And you will see me more contented
And more beautiful and more happy,
Than you have ever seen me before.

You will feel the same peace and joy that I am feeling.

Now if you can imagine this then you will understand
That death is not an ending but merely a passing
From one room to another in the mansions of time

Where there are no trials or tribulations,
Where time is not counted in years

Where there are no days,
No hours, no minutes and no tears.

For love goes on forever and love will never end.

Yvonne Goddard

If the bereaved witnessed their lost loved one fading and suffering from Alzheimer's or dementia, they may find the following reading meaningful and comforting. It can be adapted to suit an elderly gentleman, too.

The Shadow of a Woman

How do you cope when someone you hold
Most dear—suddenly dies
How do you face people, aloof, detached?
Yet mourn in silence—with unheard cries
How do you hold back the tears?
Yet folks think you're very brave
But you battle on with daily tasks
Dwelling on comforts—she once gave
How do you express the hurt, the shame?
When recognition faded … even her name.
She used to laugh, whistle and hum
Appreciate music, movies and lots of fun
Then floundered helplessly … misunderstood!
You then coped—as best you could
How do you say, you had to repeat
Patiently—things one takes for granted?
As she once housed goodness and beauty
That God had initially planted.
Each time you caressed her feeble hand

Only those who care—may understand …
She'd lost every goal, it tore your soul
That saddened, empty whole …
The laughter, the songs, the games once played
Memories of yesterday—still heavy with pain
Can never be erased …
As the Love you felt and the Love you still feel
Will always, always remain the same!

Ruth Van Gramberg (adapted)

Final tribute

As a tribute to Amelia, while we play the beautiful melody 'Amazing Grace',
would those who wish to please come forward and place your flower on the
casket, expressing your love and saying farewell.

Committal

Well, family and friends, it is now time to say our farewell to Amelia.

You closed your eyes and were taken to a beautiful place,
And left us to try to understand.

Others are taken this we know,
But you were ours and we loved you so.

You'll be in our thoughts every day,
In our hearts and you will always stay.

A silent prayer and a tear too,
We will always love you and miss you.

Go with our love, in time we'll understand
Go with our blessing, into loving, caring hands.

Author unknown

Please be upstanding.

Tenderly and reverently we commit Amelia's body to the ground.

We are grateful for the life that Amelia has lived, and for all that life has meant to us. We are glad Amelia lived.

We are glad we saw her face and felt the pressure of her hand. We cherish the memories of her words, her deeds and her character.

We cherish her friendship. And most of all we cherish her love.

Closing music

Please be seated.

As final tribute to Amelia, we will now play another of her favourite songs— one she often played on the piano at home. It's a beautiful song sung by Vera Lynn: 'We'll Meet Again'.

Benediction

We now leave the memory of our beloved Amelia in peace.

With enduring love and respect we bid her farewell, and promise her to have a devotion to things worthwhile, and make our living of real and meaningful value.

May you find richness and example in your memories of Amelia.

May you find strength and support in your love for one another, and may you find peace in your hearts.

7 *An elderly gentleman*

As in the previous sample service, I always explain to the bereaved at the time of meeting with them that the service for their elderly departed loved one is a celebration of a life well lived. Accordingly, as we will have our solemn moments, so too can we share with the mourners some light-hearted, joyous occasions in the life of the departed.

Starting the service

You might start a service for an elderly gentleman by playing appropriate music — either the choice of the bereaved or the funeral director. You could play it for 10 minutes prior to the start of the service.

An opening reading

> *Love doesn't end with dying,*
> *Or leave with the last breath.*
>
> *For someone you have loved dearly,*
> *Love goes on forever.*

Introduction

> *As you are aware, a fine gentleman has been lost to us. So we are here today to celebrate the life of Gordon Lewis.*
>
> *I ask that you please feel free to be at one with your sorrow, your sadness, your grief and your memories — but also I ask you to also feel the gladness, the happiness, the purpose and the serenity of a life so well lived.*
>
> *We are here today because Gordon Lewis found the comfort of contentment and peace. I thank you all for your presence here today, as we commemorate*

with sorrow but also with respect, joy and thankfulness the life of Gordon.

At the conclusion of the service you are invited to Fiona's place for a cup of tea and a chat, and to share those special moments you shared with Gordon.

In many ways, death unites us all for it demands that each of us put aside our toil, our business and our pleasure to unite ourselves with everyone here—fellow mourners who share in a common bond of love and respect for Gordon.

As with any funeral service, we gather to mourn a departed loved one, pay tribute to their achievements and their life, comfort one another and give our support to each other. These are not enough to soften the blow of the experience of death. We can feel a great range of emotions—anger, pain, hurt, sorrow and grief—but there is one thing that cannot be taken away, and that is the experience of loving and the experience of friendship.

When we lose someone dear to us the hurt can be almost unbearable, yet somehow we seem to get through it. And I believe that it is because we feel such pain—because the inner ache is so great—that the grief and heartache we feel bears witness to the depths of our love. You see, grief is a great indicator and measure of love. It simple cannot and does not exist except where there has been love.

I am sure that Gordon would not want you to grieve in hurt or pain, but think of the joy that he has given, that he has received and that he has shared.

Reading

I would like to read this verse, which so epitomises Gordon.

> *He has achieved success who has lived well, laughed often, and loved much*

> *Who has enjoyed the trust of pure women, the respect of intelligent men and the love of little children*

> *Who has filled his niche and accomplished his task*

> *Who has never lacked appreciation of Earth's beauty or failed to express it*

Who has left the world better than he found it
Whether an improved poppy, a perfect poem, or a rescued soul

Who has always looked for the best in others and given them the best
he had

Whose life was an inspiration
Whose memory a benediction.

Adapted from Bessie A. Stanley, 'What Constitutes Success'

Words to soften grief

We grieve today with thoughts of Gordon foremost in our minds. His passing has brought sorrow to his family and friends, particularly as the ties of love and friendship were so strong.

But while we think of Gordon's passing with sadness and regret, we should recall his life with respect and happiness. You see, nothing can detract from the happiness and closeness you shared with Gordon. Nothing can affect the happiness and the joy of life that Gordon knew. And nothing can alter your love for him and his love for you. This love can never be altered by time, circumstances or even by death. The past, with all its meaning, remains sacred and secure. It cannot be taken away.

Be grateful that Gordon was part of your lives and let his influence, his character, his warmth and his deeds live on. The following verse may be of some comfort for us all.

Don't think of him as gone away,
His journey's just begun.
Life holds so many facets;
This earth is only one.

Just think of him as resting
From the sorrow and the tears
In a place of warmth and comfort,
Where there are no days and years.

Think how he must be wishing
That we could know today
How nothing but our sadness
Can really pass away.

And think of him as living
In the hearts of those he touched,
For nothing loved is ever lost,
And he was loved so much.

Author unknown

Words for the living

I would now like to share with you some words of comfort.

For each of us here today life is a journey.
It is a journey in time.

Our birth is the beginning of that journey
And it is important to believe
That death is not the end but the destination.

For our life is a journey that takes us
From youth to age
From innocence to awareness,
From ignorance to knowledge,
From foolishness to wisdom,
From weakness to strength and often back again.

It takes us from offence to forgiveness,
From loneliness to friendship,
From pain to compassion,
From fear to faith.

From defeat to defeat to defeat,
Until looking backwards or ahead
We see that victory does not lie
At some high point along the way

But in having made the journey,
Step by step:
A sacred pilgrimage.

Author unknown

The children's tribute

Fiona, Helen and Anne loved their dad very much, and he them. They would like to share the following lovely words with us.

Dad, we want you to know that we loved you.
You were a very important part of our lives.

Our relationship, our memories and moments shared,
And the love you've given us,
Are all so very precious to us.

We count our blessings to have had a father like you,
And we hope you realised
That you have always been our inspiration.

You have guided us in each decision,
And encouraged us to reach for every dream.

You have helped us through your guidance, your wisdom
And the strength of your love,
To become the people you wanted us to be.

We want you to know
That though we may not have told you often enough,
You mean so much more to us than words can say.
We thank you and we love you with all our hearts.

Author unknown

Eulogy

For the next few minutes, it will be my privilege to share with you the life of Gordon Lewis.

As well as sharing in Gordon's life we also share in our grief at his passing. And, speaking with the family, it is clear they would not want you to grieve in hurt or pain, but concentrate on the joy that Gordon has given, that Gordon has received and that Gordon has shared.

Gordon Peter Lewis was born at Dunkeld, Victoria, on the edge of the Grampians, on the 18th of September 1920. Gordon's parents were Albert and Millie and he had a brother, Ron, now deceased. When he was young the family moved to Ballarat, where Gordon attended school at the local state high school. After leaving school—well, actually he didn't ever really leave school—he embarked on a wonderful career that was to embrace 40 years in the teaching profession.

Gordon's career was put on hold as he joined up to serve in World War II. He enlisted in the army in 1942. While stationed in the Middle East he became ill and returned home to Australia. Gordon was one of those unsung heroes who sacrificed those early years of his life serving his country. He was discharged from the army in 1946.

By the time Gordon joined up, he had already met Gladys, his wife to be, through mutual friends at Ballarat. During their courtship, Gordon and Gladys had lots of fun rowing on the lake, going to the movies and riding their bicycles. They got up to a bit of mischief, too—late at night, after the pictures ended, they'd sneak down to the back of the local pub and give the secret knock to allow them entry. And of course they fell in love, and were married just before Gordon joined the army, at St Bridget's Church, on the 19th of June 1942. Thus began a wonderful togetherness, which saw the celebration of a golden wedding anniversary. Their marriage was blessed by three daughters: Fiona, Helen and Anne.

Gordon's pride and joy were his grandchildren—he was pa to Sarah, Peter, Janine and Tamara. He loved them dearly, and they him. And Gordon was also the very proud great-grandpa to Liam and Emily. Gordon saw that his children had a wonderful, happy upbringing and that they were afforded every opportunity, and that quality of parenthood has been followed through by his grandchildren. They had many wonderful holidays with Gordon and Gladys, and can well remember riding the ponies and swimming in the dam with their pa.

Gordon had a distinguished career in the teaching profession. After his discharge from the army in 1946 he began a humanities degree at Melbourne University and graduated in 1948 in history and literature. He taught at Acres Hill High, Wollonga High—where he was the principal—and took the opportunity of three years' teaching on Christmas Island in the Pacific, which he greatly enjoyed.

Returning to Australia, he then made his mark at Camptown High, then at Landsvale High as principal. In this role he immediately impressed the community with his energy, vision and clear-sighted understanding of the demands of the position.

He was gentle in his dealings with colleagues, students, parents and with the wider community. He was a man who stood firmly by his principles, morals and ethical beliefs. He had a fundamental decency that shone like a beacon through the good times and the bad, and was remembered long after Gordon retired from Landsvale High in 1981.

Gordon had many interests. He enjoyed golf, reducing his handicap on his favourite courses and relishing his one after-game drink in the clubhouse with his friends. He was also a very competent cricketer, and loved watching Aussie Rules on the TV—barracking for Essendon, the Bombers. He also watched the cricket and, in fact, was knowledgeable about most sports.

Gordon enjoyed gardening, growing both flowers and food, and his fruit trees at his Ballarat home were a wonderful delight, especially the citrus trees that produced seemingly endless baskets of lemons and limes. Visitors to Gladys and Gordon's house were often given a bag of delicious goodies to take home.

A special time in Gordon and Gladys's life was also spent at 'Forestglen', their country property on the Ferntree River, where they lived for eight years. The family can well remember the happy times they spent at the property. When keeping up with Forestglen became too demanding, Gordon and Gladys moved back to Ballarat, in 1990. They had a lovely house with a swimming pool and a beautiful garden. Four years ago, without the family having to tell Gordon to slow down, he and Gladys moved to the nearby Begonia Glade Retirement Village.

His other hobbies included playing—and winning!—all the classic card games, and he taught all his grandchildren how to win at cards. In fact I'm told never to take on his granddaughter, Tamara, at gin rummy, unless prepared to be beaten. He was also an avid reader, a pastime he picked up during his years in the army. His longtime friend from those wartime days, Len Simmons—who is here today—remembers how he could read his way through sirens, meals and even near-darkness!

Gordon's warm and friendly personality drew others to him and he made many friends from all walks of life, so it's no surprise that he gave generously of his time, heart, mind and spirit in service to the community. He was an active member of his local Lions Club and the Freemasons, and anyone who he thought needed help—or anyone who asked—was welcomed with loving support.

Gordon's health began to decline in the last five years of his life. He fought off several serious illnesses with his characteristic optimism, but last December became gravely ill and was given just a short time to live. Even so, his fight and his courage shone through to the last, and he spent the last month with his friends and family, always looking on the bright side and setting a wonderful example to those who cared for him. In the last week of his illness, he was admitted to St Margaret's Hospital and was lost to us last Tuesday, his family by his side in a room full of love.

On behalf of the Lewis family I would like to thank the palliative care nurses—Leanne and Margie, who are here today—whose dedication and compassion enabled Gordon to stay at home for his last weeks. And I'd also like to thank the nurses at St Margaret's for taking such wonderful care of him in his final days—you are very, very special people. Gordon's family also wish to thank Dr Penshurst and Dr Kaczala for their professional care and for treating Gordon with respect and dignity.

Gordon was a gentle person—a gentleman. He was a man not to be fussed over, nor was he to be praised. Everyone remembers how embarrassed he would become at birthday celebrations, and how often he was heard to say, 'A man should only get attention when he's done something worthwhile'. Well, Gordon's whole life was worthwhile, and remembering that will help us in our sorrow at his passing.

He valued the things that make up a person of impeccable character: sincerity, integrity, fairness, kindness and hard work. He was a loving husband, an untiring worker, a provider, an inspirational father, and a loving, generous and caring grandfather. He took each of the roles in his life seriously, giving them the importance they deserve. He lived for his family and liked nothing better than having them around him. His unique strength, his caring, his understanding and, most importantly, his capacity for always being there when he was needed are things everyone will remember.

In his professional life, Gordon was a man of scholarship, with great communication skills—loved and respected by his peers, and unselfishly dedicating his working life to passing on knowledge and wisdom to the many students that his life touched.

Gordon was a diligent, upright and warm-hearted person; a justifiably proud Australian, who served his country with great distinction; and a man who leaves behind a legacy of kindness, commitment, love and enduring respect for all those who were privileged to have known him.

You know, some men go through life never seen, never heard and never laying a brick. But Gordon has been seen, he has been heard, and he has laid the lifelong foundations for many lives in his significant contribution to his family and his community.

Readings and tributes

Family and friends

If there is anyone else here who would like to say a few words, please come forward. [Family members and friends read their tributes.]

The Lord's Prayer

For those of you who wish to, please join me in saying 'The Lord's Prayer'.

> *Our Father, which art in heaven.*
> *Hallowed be thy name.*
> *Thy Kingdom come.*
> *Thy will be done, on Earth*
> *As it is in heaven.*
> *Give us this day our daily bread.*
> *And forgive us our trespasses*
> *As we forgive those who trespass against us.*
> *And lead us not into temptation*

But deliver us from evil.
For thine is the Kingdom,
The power and the glory,
For ever and ever.

Amen.

Music

As a tribute to Gordon, we will now play the song 'Bless This House' sung by Perry Como. While this is playing, you may like to turn the pages of your memory like a book, and remember the special times you spent with Gordon.

Readings

There is a very special reading that I read to people I think are quite special. Some of you may have heard it before, but today I read it for you, Gordon's and his friends. For Gordon was a very special man. It is called The Dash.

[This poem, written by Linda Ellis, can be found at www.lindaslyrics.com/thedashpoem.html]

When someone we love dies, we are faced with trying to understand one of life's great mysteries. But I believe the following words are a way of looking at death that is comforting, and that makes it just a little easier to understand.

One at Rest

Think of me as one at rest,
For me you should not weep
I have no pain no troubled thoughts
For I am just asleep.
The living thinking me that was,
Is now forever still
And life goes on without me now,
As time forever will.

If your heart is heavy now
Because I've gone away
Dwell not long upon it, friend
For none of us can stay.
Those of you who liked me,
I sincerely thank you all
And those of you who loved me,
I thank you most of all.

And in my fleeting lifespan,
As time went rushing by
I found some time to hesitate,
To laugh, to love, to cry.
Matters it now if time began,
If time will ever cease?
I was here, I used it all,
And now I am at peace.

Author unknown

Committal

Well, family and friends, the time has come to say our farewell to Gordon.

I have got to leave you.
Bid me farewell, my family and my friends.

I bow to you all and take my departure,
Here I give back the keys to the door.

I give up all claims to my house,
I ask only kind words from you.

We were neighbours, family and friends for so long,
But I have received more than I could give.

Now the day has dawned,
And the lamp that lit my dark corner is out.

A summons has come,
And I am ready for the journey.

Author unknown

Before we say farewell to Gordon, let us be grateful once more for the tangibles—the impact of Gordon's life on yours. Each of you will remember the good times you spent with him, and the times you struggled and searched with him. You will remember Gordon's love for you, his love of life, and your love for him.

Please be upstanding.

Tenderly and reverently we commit Gordon's body to be cremated.

We are grateful for the life that has been lived, and for all that life has meant to us. We are glad Gordon lived. We are glad we saw his face and felt the pressure of his hand. We cherish the memories of his words, his deeds and his character.

We cherish his friendship. And most of all we cherish his love.

Closing music

Please be seated.

As a final tribute to Gordon we will now play the beautiful song, 'Time to Say Goodbye' sung by Andrea Bocelli and Sarah Brightman.

Final reading

These are some final words I say to you from Gordon.

Miss me — but let me go

When I come to the end of the road,
And the sun has set for me,
I want no rites in a gloom-filled room.
Why cry for a soul set free?

Miss me a little — but not too long
and not with your head bowed low,
Remember the love that we once shared.
Miss me — but let me go.

For this is a journey we all must take,
And each must go alone.
It's all part of the master plan,
A step on the road to home.

When you are lonely and sick of heart,
Go to the friends we know.
Bury your sorrows in doing good deeds.
Miss me — but let me go.

Author unknown

Benediction

We now leave the memory of our beloved Gordon in peace.

With enduring love and respect we bid him farewell. And let us promise him to have a devotion to things worthwhile and fill our own lives with words and actions of real and meaningful worth.

May you find richness and example in your memories of Gordon. May you find strength and support in your love for one another. And may you find peace in your hearts.

8 *Tragic deaths*

Funerals can be tragic affairs for the family and friends of the deceased, but never is this more so than when unexpected deaths occur and people are taken before their time, with so much more to offer.

At these times, the bereaved will be struggling with powerful emotions, and will have trouble expressing themselves. Great care should be taken to respect the painful grieving of family and friends and to focus, if you can, on the person who has been lost. A funeral services for someone who has died tragically should concentrate on the parts of the deceased's life that can be celebrated and shared, rather than the manner of their passing.

In this chapter we'll look at a some sample services for some of these tragic deaths. We'll begin with a man whose health failed him in his mid-thirties; consider the sudden death of a teenager and a service for a suicide; think about how to approach the family of a murder victim; and look at some appropriate readings for a lonely death. Each service demands a unique, individual approach, but such circumstances as these also require particular sensitivity and understanding from the celebrant.

To avoid unnecessary repetition, we're going to skip over the reasonably generic parts of a funeral service—see the previous services in Chapters 6 and 7 for these. Instead we're going to leap straight into the heart of each service and look at the particulars of each case, and the special way the eulogies and specific readings might be handled to deal with the sudden nature of these passings.

Service for a young man

A young country man, Luke, was 36 years old, happily married, a father of one, and seemingly a picture of good health before being struck down with illness and passing away. I was called on to be the celebrant for this service, and it has stuck with me as an especially poignant one for the sense of loss and shock in his community and amongst Luke's family and friends.

The opening stages of the funeral comprised an introduction, some opening readings and several musical tributes that were selected by the family. In a situation like this, I prefer to focus on celebrating the deceased's life and loves. While not shirking the manner of the untimely death, neither do I tend to dwell upon this and lose sight of celebrating the person's life.

Eulogy (extract)

Luke met Chrissy at a dance in Birdsville, and I'm told on good authority it was love at first sight. They both loved dancing and the great outdoors. Their marriage was a wonderful togetherness and one which brought love and happiness to many others. The birth of their son, Connor, two years ago brought immense joy to them, and Luke loved being a dad more than anything else.

Luke was a gifted sportsman with a heart as big as Phar Lap. We have heard about his great football career but a few years ago Luke also turned his skills to rodeos, competing in Windorah and Mount Isa. He also loved a joke and had a wonderful sense of humour, as we've heard, but what we've not mentioned was that when Luke and his good mate Sam got together it was always a riot.

Luke enjoyed the movies, particularly the classics and his favourite film star, Cary Grant. He had almost every record that Dean Martin made and could impersonate him brilliantly, especially when his family and friends egged him on to sing 'That's Amore'.

Luke was such a fit person that it came as a shock to his family and friends when about 18 months ago he became ill. With treatment he recovered, but just three months ago his health deteriorated again, and last week he was admitted to hospital. Sadly it was there that Luke was lost to us last Thursday, his family by his side in a room full of love.

The spirit, dignity and courage that marked Luke's life were never more evident than right at the very end. Without complaining, he never gave up, and always had a special word and great big hug for anyone who came to visit. And the family would like to thank Dr Everett at the Mercy Hospital, and all the nurses who cared for Luke, for the devotion they extended to Luke in his final weeks.

Luke was a loving husband, a hard worker, a good provider, a committed and generous father, and an energetic uncle to his nieces and nephews. He was a man who lived for his family and thus made sure that his family was afforded every opportunity. He was rewarded with their love and he liked nothing better than having them around him.

In his work as a mechanic, Luke was always dedicated to the task, and always had a friendly word for a customer or workmate. He was a man whose warm and friendly personality drew others to him and he made countless friends from all walks of life. He loved nothing more than helping out a mate or a stranded traveller, sitting them down with a cuppa, having a chat and going out of his way to fix whatever needed fixing. The postcards he received from grateful strangers, pinned to the wall of the garage, are a testament to the effect he had on others.

Luke was a man who added value to the things he was dedicated to. He was someone who could turn something ordinary into something extraordinary. His greatness was not achieved or measured in terms of wealth or fame, but in strength of heart, courage and spirit.

Luke was a true, diligent, upright and proud Australian who has left behind a legacy of kindness, love and commitment and enduring respect from all who were privileged to have known him. To the world Luke was but one man, but to his family he was the world.

Music

One of Luke's favourite songs was 'Everybody Loves Somebody Sometime' by Dean Martin. While it is playing, you might like to turn the pages of your memory like a book, remembering the special times you spent with Luke.

A special reading

As always, I invited the family to select readings and music that would have suited their loved one.

You Will Always Be There

*The rays of light filtered through the sentinels of
trees this morning.
I sat in the garden and contemplated.*

*The serenity and beauty of my feelings and
surroundings completely captivated me …
I thought of you.*

I discovered you tucked away in the shadows
of the trees.
Then rediscovered you, on the smiles of the flowers
As the sun penetrated the petals …
In the rhythm of the leaves falling in the garden …
In the freedom of the birds as they fly
Searching as you do …

I'm very happy to have found you …
Now you will never leave me for I will always find you
In the beauty of life.

Author unknown

Committal

At this stage in the proceedings, although I had other readings, as there was not a dry eye in the chapel I thought the timing was right for the committal. As always, I tried to have more material than I needed. The aim of many of the readings and songs was to prepare the bereaved for the committal but by this time they seemed ready for it. I find it helps to be flexible enough to add items in or drop them out of a service as required.

Well, family and friends, the time has come to say our farewell to Luke.

I have got to leave you,
bid me farewell, my friends, my family.

I bow to you all and take my departure,
I have come to the end of the road
And the sun has set for me.

I want no tears in a gloom-filled room.
Why cry for a soul set free?

For to live in the hearts of those we love is not to die.
Miss me, but let me go.

Miss me a little, but not for long
And not with your head bowed low.
Remember the joy and love that once was shared.
Memory is the treasury and keeper of all things.
Miss me, but let me go.

For this is a journey we must all take.
A summons has come and I am ready for the journey
As each must go alone.
Miss me, but let me go.

Please be upstanding.

Tenderly and reverently we commit Luke's body to the ground. We are grateful for the life that has been lived and for all that his life has meant to us. We are glad Luke lived. We are glad we saw his face and felt the pressure of his hand. We cherish the memories of his words, his deeds and his character.

We cherish his friendship. And most of all we cherish his love.

Closing music

Please be seated.

As a final tribute to Luke we will now play one of his favourite songs, 'Love Me Tender' by Elvis Presley.

Service for a teenager

Let's move ahead to another tragic circumstance. If the untimely death of a 36-year-old taken before his time is an emotional and tragic event, the death of a teenager is even more tragic for the extra time lost, an adult life untouched and a life's potential unrealised.

In this example, Jessica was killed in a tragic drowning accident, aged 19. A picture board was placed in the foyer of the chapel featuring many photos of Jessica's life. A table at the front of the chapel displayed a photo of Jessica and some of her favourite things—her hockey stick, her favourite book, the beautiful dress she'd designed and made herself for her school formal only eighteen months before. The chapel was filled with young people from the local community, her friends from school and her family.

Opening words

We are here today because the loved daughter of Janice and Simon, sister of Lauren, has tragically left us.

Our grief and sorrow is all the more painful by the passing of such a young woman. You see, when the elderly depart we recognise a natural change. It feels normal—the end of a lifetime and life span encompassing all that was to be given and achieved. But the passing of such a young person shocks us. It seems so unfair, so needless, a waste of a life that had so much to give—mountains to climb, rivers to cross, challenges to be faced and conquered.

I speak of Jessica Woodley, born in Sydney on the 20th of September 1989— just 19 years of age.

We grieve today with thoughts of Jessica foremost in our minds. Her passing has brought sorrow to her family and friends, particularly as the ties of love and friendship were so strong. But while we think of Jessica's passing with sadness and regret, we should recall her life with respect and happiness.

You see, nothing can ever change the happiness and closeness you shared with Jessica. Nothing can affect the joy of life that Jessica knew. Nothing can come between your love for her and her love for you. The past that you and Jessica shared can never alter. It is forever sacred and secure.

Be grateful that Jessica was part of your lives and let her influence, her character, her lovely warmth and her deeds live on.

Some words of comfort

Life does proceed when a loved one leaves.
But it's difficult for us who are left to grieve.

We'll pick ourselves up and try again.
We'll make the effort to function again.

It won't be easy, as we well know.
But we won't give up—the change made us grow.

We loved Jessica so much, and fate was unkind.
She went away first, she left us behind.

The pain in our hearts will remain yet awhile.
But yesterday's gone. Tomorrow we'll try to smile.

Author unknown

Music

As you entered the chapel you heard music by Powderfinger, one of Jessica's favourite bands. Another favourite artist was Missy Higgins, and we will now play her song 'Going North'.

Tributes

Jessica will now be honoured by two speakers. Firstly, Petra, the coach of Jessica's under-19s hockey team, will share some thoughts. Then we will hear from Lauren, Jessica's sister. [The speakers then present their tributes.]

Eulogy (extract)

As well as sharing in Jessica's life we also share our grief at her passing. But speaking with her lovely family, they would not want you to grieve in hurt or pain but grieve in the joy and love that Jessica has given, that Jessica has received and that Jessica has shared.

Let's start by saying thank you to Jessica for the joy and love of her infancy. She was a happy little mischief-maker, never worried about getting her hands dirty. She loved making noise—the saucepan lids were her favourite toys, and playing games with the family border collies came a close second.

Throughout her short life, Jessica was the sort of person who could solve any problem or help any friend in need. The countless times she helped a friend sew an outfit for a special occasion, or gave people lifts in her beloved, battered red Toyota, or looked after anyone who needed looking after will all be remembered forever.

So let's say thank you to Jessica for all she did to earn the reputation she had as a kind and loving friend. Her countless friends—and there are many of you here today—have personal reasons to know what that means. So we say thank you to Jessica for being such a caring friend to the really special people in her life. She loved keeping in touch with her family and friends. When she was overseas she'd ring her mum and dad to tell them how much she was missing them. And more than once they received a surprise gift, posted from overseas, which showed how much Jessica was thinking of them.

I then continued on to speak of other aspects of Jessica's caring and active life.

A special meaning from the tragedy

I believe we should say thank you to Jessica for the new awareness that has manifested even since her tragic death—awareness of family, friends, workmates and team members.

I can't help feeling that there is something special about today. You see, you are the positive evidence that Jessica's influence hasn't just ceased because she has left us. In some special way she has even more strength now to bring people together, to touch something deep down in us.

You can't help feeling that there's something special Jessica wants to say to us. Something different to each one of us, according to our strengths and the different parts we played in her life.

For some, it may be not to put off what you want to do in life. For some, to give more of ourselves to others like she did. For some, not to take life too seriously because you never know how brief it might be. For others, to take life more seriously because it is so fragile.

For all of us, it may be that we need to reassess our values and priorities, and recognise how trivial the things that divide us are. Or it might be to attend to the little things that really are the big things, like telling people how much they mean to us, how much we appreciate them, even how much we love them before it's too late. Jessica might even be challenging us to make our own lives more meaningful and worthwhile.

And if we can do this, what we are really doing for Jessica is giving continuing purpose to her life, some meaning to her passing and a living and lasting stake in our lives. So then Jessica will not just be part of the past in our memories, or of the present in our grief, but very much part of our future lives. Through all these things that we have learned from her life and added to our own for the benefit of all, Jessica's spirit will be very much alive.

And then, some day, looking back, we will see Jessica's memory, not as it is today—a tear-filled cloud—but as a beautiful light on our horizon, giving our life an extra richness and dimension of meaning.

Jessica was a kind, tolerant, enthusiastic, courteous and friendly young woman who had an innate decency and integrity. She had a great sense of humour, a mischievous smile, and a laugh that couldn't help but be contagious. She never flinched in a crisis, never ducked for cover, and was always consistent in her manner and life. She was a gifted hockey player, and always gave her best not just for herself but for the team. And so it is today that we grieve the loss of a young woman who in her short stay on Earth has given so much and had so much more to give.

As a tribute to Jessica I ask you all to be upstanding for one minute in silent prayer or in reflection of the special times you spent with your lost family member or friend.

I then read the 23rd Psalm, as requested by Jessica's family. This was followed by a pre-committal reading (see Chapter 4) followed by the committal ceremony. I then closed with a benediction.

Service for a suicide

In the case of a suicide the feelings of the family will dictate the mood of the service. Emotions are confused and the decision of what information to disclose is a difficult one. Many families do not want any reference to the fact that it their loved one's death was a suicide. Other families ask you to refer to the nature of the death, but in brief terms. In both instances one must respect the wishes of the family.

Don't be surprised by the intensity of feeling. Accept that the survivors may be struggling with explosive emotions—guilt, fear, anger and shame—well beyond those experienced in other types of death. So when conducting the interview you must be especially patient, compassionate and understanding.

In some cases where it was well known to family and friends that the deceased had suffered painful bouts of depression for some years, I have gently suggested to the bereaved family that communicating the facts of their loved one's death might help to open up communication with the mourners. In such cases, the atmosphere of tense, serious-looking mourners changed to one of relief, with people able to unite with each other in warmth, tears and love—not only for the lost one but for the family.

The suicide—or you may wish to say 'ending of a life'—can either be mentioned in the introductory remarks or be included early in the eulogy. Either way, the eulogy should still be centred on the life, aspirations, joys, achievements and loves of the deceased. Personally, I prefer to have the facts out of the way so the mourners can feel more comfortable in their sharing of grief.

If you have the family's approval, name the circumstances but do not allow them to overshadow the primary purpose of the service, which is to honour their loved one's life.

In nearly every case of suicide, the feeling of guilt is strong among family members and close friends. I make a point of impressing upon the family and friends that in no way should they burden themselves with such feelings. I reassure them that even though they think they could have done more, it would not have changed the course of events. People have choices, and a person's tragic decision to end their life should not put blame onto others.

Opening words

After greeting those in attendance, if it's acceptable to the family you can say something like the following.

> We gather to honour Cameron's memory and to support one another in grieving
> a death that is the hardest death to grieve: death that is chosen.

Life is full of suffering. To the beloved gathered here today has come a grief and loss that strains the ability to bear—to endure the enormity of it and go on.

In the midst of brokenness and broken-heartedness, may we know the grace of love that sustains us—love that endures beyond death. May there be peace and healing. May there be acceptance that Cameron—beloved son, husband and brother—chose his healing into death.

May all who must somehow find the courage to continue to face life in the face of this loss receive the grace of healing into life. May we affirm all that was good and true and generous and beautiful in the life of Cameron.

May we affirm the love in which he was conceived and nurtured and sent forth, an autonomous human being who made his own decision, as we all must do.

This heart that breaks open can contain the whole world.

Keep breathing. Trust that your heart is large enough.

Let us speak together. Let us grieve together as we share memories of Cameron and all that he meant in the lives of those here.

Eulogy (extract)

We gather here to mourn the loss of Cameron, each with our own feelings of grief. We gather to hold up his memory, and to say goodbye.

Our tears of sadness for a loss of a life that was maturing and blossoming mingle with the tears of possibilities, rivers to cross, mountains to climb, challenges to be faces and conquered.

Cameron's free and untamed spirit, which he chose to end, will be forever in our memories.

I ask that no one should feel bruised by Cameron's decision and please cease asking yourselves what you could have done. Cameron's decision came from a struggle within himself—he knew the moments of life that were cherished in joy, friendship, achievement, sharing and love, just as he also knew the painful bouts of depression that intermittently entered his life.

The illness of mood swings and the pain derived from such is probably the cruellest pain of all. It is something almost incurable—leading neurosurgeons and medical science are unable to find a cure or answer.

One minute, a person is bright, happy and content; the next, a mind is commanded by anxiety, self-doubt and dreaded depression. Unlike other pains, it is not confined to a limb or an organ but pervades the whole being, affecting every relationship and endeavour.

Treatment is not clear-cut or effective and perhaps, worst of all, depression claims not only the sufferer but others who love and care for that person. Here was Cameron, filled with joy just a week ago at his brother Karl's birthday. Here was Cameron, conversing and laughing happily with his friends at a barbecue just last weekend. And then, just a short time after that happy event, his illness led him to make a fatal decision.

If it is difficult to accept Cameron's final decision then please consider this. Cameron had a tormenting illness, but for eight years he bravely faced a terrible struggle which none of us can even begin to comprehend. It is therefore so important, so imperative for you to realise that there can be no blame whatsoever on the shoulders of others.

Here I am reminded of the words spoken by St Francis of Assisi:

May we have the serenity to accept the things we cannot change, courage to change the things we can, and wisdom to know the difference.

Now I have talked a lot in this eulogy about the illness, but it's important to not let this overshadow a celebration of a life lived, loves and friendships shared, and other positive aspects that remind the bereaved why they loved their lost one so dearly. Here it's important to speak of the deceased's life—birth, schooling, occupation, family life, sport, hobbies, interests and flirtations.

Following this I might conclude with something along the following lines:

Cameron's life, although cut short, was lived to the full. But the scars of life that led Cameron to make his choice were wounds that we will never know and that Cameron did not find the inner strength to heal. How long he lived with the pain that he contained within himself should be admired by us, for never was he known to have cast a stone or uttered a bad word about anyone.

The last eight years of Cameron's life were not easy but with stoical courage he faced life bravely, endeavouring to look on the bright side. Sadly, last Tuesday Cameron was lost to us. Cameron loved his family dearly and treasured the wonderful times they shared. Always in their memories will be that mischievious chuckle and that gentle voice.

He will be sadly missed by those whose lives he touched and those who loved him. Most importantly, he will be missed for who he was, and the courage he showed to live life the way he chose.

A mother and father enduring similar pain to what you are today once wrote:

The memories of you, our son, will never die.
Even though you chose to close your eyes.

Our love for you lives on, our son
Just as we choose to go on living as one.

Maybe you did give us a gift unknowingly,
And that is to learn to live again—fully and completely.

The pain of losing you will always be there.
But there comes a time to let go and say goodbye.

In our hearts you will stay forever and a day.
Farewell, we'll love you always.

Author unknown, **The Compassionate Friends (Victoria) Magazine**, *2003*

For some years Cameron's loved ones had noticed that his actions, his depression and his withdrawal from the world were unlike the Cameron that they knew. They only knew him as an enthusiastic participant in life, taking every opportunity that came his way.

So it is important that through this sadness and disbelief that we feel, we remember his zest for the adventures of life, his raucous laughter, his dry sense of humour, his warmth and the kindness that radiated from him. The joy of friendship and family which dominated his short life will live forever in the lives of his loved ones much longer than the choice he made in the end.

Now, to farewell Cameron, we say to him:

> *You tried so hard, you told so few*
> *We will never know what you went through.*

> *You never failed to do your best*
> *Your heart was true and tender*
> *You simply lived for those you loved*
> *And those you loved will remember.*

Author unknown

Service for a victim of murder

Like the loss of life by suicide, how can one express, soften or even address the feeling of a bereaved family when a life is lost through murder? It takes the utmost of care to approach a funeral under such terrible circumstances. In many cases, the service may be almost like a therapy session.

Family members overwhelmingly feel disbelief. They feel numb and distrustful of life. Even the act of grieving seems a forlorn one for it won't bring back their loved one lost so suddenly.

Needless to say, on the occasions when I've had to interview families after a murder to gain sufficient information for a meaningful eulogy, it has been extremely difficult. Some people may resent being asked to relive the life of the deceased; their understandable bitterness, anger and desire for revenge need to be approached with delicacy and extreme tact. As with suicides, the bereaved are dealing with their own personal emotions and struggling with rage and despair. Always be prepared for relatives and friends to make inappropriate remarks — they will be experiencing strong feelings and will have difficulty expressing themselves.

No matter what their reactions, try to be a loving friend and listen to their feelings. If faith is part of their lives, they may be mad at God. If they are mad at God, encourage them to talk about it. If they name the murderer, or focus on revenge, try to take the focus off that person to concentrate on recording material about the life of the deceased.

'Robbed of life' was the catchphrase that kept coming back during the interviews I've conducted under these circumstances. The world of these families had been shattered—not more so than any other family facing the loss of their loved one, but the circumstances of the death made the situation so much more difficult.

I have conducted three murder services. Obviously these services will all be very different, and cover very senstive territory. Try to address the emotion and not the specific circumstances of the death in the service, but be very mindful of the feelings of the bereaved—loss, shattering grief and outrage. Accordingly I endeavour to treat the actual service as if a normal passing, however if requested by the family to refer to the nature of the death I do so briefly, in a quite open way. I use a shortened introduction, standard verses such as 'One at Rest' and 'The Lord's Prayer' if requested. I find my normal committal appropriate.

To put together a service, I suggest you draw appropriate readings from Part 2 of the book, and try to share the eulogy with other speakers to provide a broad view of the life and personality of the deceased.

Service for a lonely death

Occasionally you will conduct a service in which the deceased has no immediate family and sometimes few friends. Those who have led a solitary life and cut themselves off from society, as some are wont to do, may die alone.

At the beginning of such a service I ask those friends and acquaintances who have come to pay respects to 'become' the deceased's family. And I always include the following beautiful reading about friendship.

> *Thank you for being a friend to me,*
> *When I needed someone there,*
> *My failing hopes to bolster,*
> *And my secret fears to share.*

> *Thank you for being so good to me,*
> *When it was hard to know*
> *The wisest course to follow,*
> *What to do and where to go.*

> *Thank you for giving me confidence*
> *When I had lost the way,*
> *Speaking the word that led me through*
> *The course of the day.*

Thank you for all you did and said
To ease the weight for me,
Never intruding but always there
In the background, helping quietly.

Thank you not only for sympathy
In times of grief and stress,
But for all you have meant to me
In terms of happiness.

Many a lovely day we've known,
And many a laugh we've had.
Thank you for being my friend.

Author unknown

Another suitable verse when the deceased has few family and friends is the following.

The rich and the poor listen to the voice of death,
The learned and the learned listen.

The proud and the humble listen.
The honest and the deceitful listen.
The old and the young listen.

But the voice of death speaks to us.
What does it say?

Death does not say, 'Fear me',
It does not say, 'Wonder at me'.

It does not say 'Understand me',
But it says to us, 'Think of life,
Think of the privilege of life,
Think how great a thing life may be.'

Author unknown

I have had occasion to conduct a service for a person not well respected and fallen on hard times, with few family members and friends if any in attendance. I have found the following reading appropriate in those circumstances.

Pray don't find fault with the man who limps,
Or stumbles along the road,
Unless you have worn the shoes he wears,
Or struggled beneath his load.

There may be tacks in his shoes that hurt,
Though hidden away from view,
Or the burden he bears placed on your neck,
Might cause you to stumble too.

Don't sneer at the man's who's down today,
Unless you have felt the blow
That caused his fall, or felt the shame
That only the fallen know.

You may be strong, but still the blows
That were his, if dealt to you
In the selfsame way at the selfsame time,
Might cause you to stagger, too.

Don't be too harsh with the man who sins,
Or pelt him with words or stones,
Unless you are sure, yes, double sure,
That you have not sins of your own.

For you know, perhaps, if the tempter's voice
Should whisper as soft as you,
As it did to him when he went astray,
Would cause you to falter, too.

Author unknown

Reading for a drug-related death

The following is a poignant reading which might be used when someone has lost their life to drugs. It can be adapted to suit the particular sad occasion.

One So Beloved

Through anguished, tear-filled years, love remains
And memories rustle the pages of one sweet life
The unanswered 'whys?' that were uttered
In frustrated plea, so frequently
Whilst loving hearts perceived that he was special
His life had cruel limitations.
In a kaleidoscope of pills and potions he manifested
Light and dark, fire and spirit, understanding, ambition
Persuasion and perseverance
Acknowledging neither defeat nor self-pity
Steadfastly pursuing excellence
His youth disappearing in molten dreams
'twixt days awash with tears and silent pain
An odyssey of pierced veins and bruised seams
Yet his smiles belied the turbulence.
Though small, he stood so very tall with countenance
That masked a tortured spirit
Thus bravely, loving expansively, 'midst the miasma
Of drips and drugs and alien hospice
He clung to hope, though his stay on earth was done
And peace—his rightful due.
A camouflage of mindless hours and anguished minutes
Once fettered, springing free, as patterned lives
Move on—another page is turned
Come one, come all—kiss all strife goodbye and smile
For having known him!

Ruth Van Gramberg

9 Infant deaths

What do you do when approached to conduct a service for a baby that has only lived a matter of days, hours or even minutes? The death of a baby is a unique challenge for a funeral celebrant, as the usual practice of focusing on a life lived, and celebrating good times and experiences shared, does not apply. Instead we are faced with the challenge of creating a meaningful ritual to mark the loss of a life unlived, of good times that were never shared and of a life that was expected but cruelly cut short.

If we are able to connect with the grieving parents and family and to examine their expectations and the love that they shared with their baby in preparing for his or her arrival, it is possible to mark the occasion and to prepare a service every bit as meaningful as that for a life long lived.

The first time this situation occurred for me as a celebrant, I initially felt entirely inadequate for the task. What words of comfort could I possibly find for such a sad and intensely emotional occasion—the death of baby who had only lived a few hours? But by focusing on the love that had already been given and received, the grieving parents and I wrote a service together that was powerful and meaningful.

In this situation it is a great help to the parents to be active in planning the service, selecting readings and prayers. I believe this can help them through the first stages of grief; by participating in the service, they are able to channel their grief into meaningful activity rather than inwardly containing it.

This chapter offers a sample service and some thoughts for performing services in these deeply sad circumstances.

Service for an infant

Opening remarks

> *Patrick and Meredith, our deepest sorrow goes out to you today. We all know how you were waiting to be wonderful, caring parents. To baby Zoe's grandparents—Harry, Lena, Greg and Diane—and to all the caring people here today who have supported Patrick and Meredith through this heart-wrenching time in their life, our thoughts are with you all.*

We know that Zoe would have brought so much love into this world, and has done so already, and you have been part of that love with your positive feelings, your caring, your concerns and in strength of your unity in family and friendship.

Meredith and Patrick are so grateful for your love and support: Meredith's brother Peter and his wife Rani, who drove back and forth to Brisbane, bringing family support at a crucial time; Patrick's friends Ben and James, who shared their home when family members needed a place to stay close to the hospital; and so many more dedicated friends and family who gave emotional and practical support during this difficult time.

Patrick and Meredith would also like to thank the staff at Prince William Hospital, whose devotion to baby Zoe and wonderful care was truly appreciated.

Scripture reading

This short reading comes from the Gospel of St Luke, chapter 18, verses 15–17.

The people were bringing infants to Jesus so that he might touch them. When the disciples saw it, they rebuked them. But Jesus called them to him, saying, 'Let the children come to me, and do not hinder them; for the kingdom of God belongs to such as these'.

Reading

At this point, a non-religious reading to provide comfort may be appropriate. For example, Edgar A. Guest's poem 'To All Parents' might be used, with some modifications to soften it and make it more appropriate for the particular situation. You can find this poem on many internet sites.

Eulogy

On behalf of Patrick and Meredith and the family of baby Zoe Olivia McDonald, I thank everyone for your presence here today. Death has a way of uniting us all, and Zoe's passing means that each of us will put aside our cares, our business and our pleasure to bring support to Meredith and Patrick.

We grieve today with thoughts of baby Zoe in our minds. There are no words of comfort that can adequately cushion the shock of this precious baby's loss to us. There does not seem to be any point in searching for the meaning of such a death. You will feel anger and pain, hurt and deep sorrow that such a thing can happen.

Yet there is one thing that can never be taken away and that is the experience of loving. Love led to baby Zoe's conception. Love flowed from the hearts of those who waited for her arrival with Meredith and Patrick. Love surrounds us all now, even though Zoe is no longer with us. She lived and breathed for only 8 hours and 17 minutes, but for every second she breathed in the love of her family beside her.

Her passing makes us see the most precious gift we have—this treasure of love. And when we lose someone we love deeply, we will feel pain like no other. It is the tears of love that flow longest, the pain of love that aches deepest, the thoughts of love that move us the most.

Many people that I talk to believe that being strong and brave about a lost loved one means trying to think and talk about something else, to distract ourselves from grief. But we know that being strong and brave means thinking and talking about our lost one. The name of your loved one is a magic word. Speak it, think it and remember it—baby Zoe lived, and in your hearts and minds she will continue to live.

*So, whatever happens, let it happen—even the tears and the sorrow. You see, it's okay to cry, it's good to cry, and it's important to express our love in this way. So speak and think of your precious Zoe until your sorrow begins to be bearable and slowly heal. Now **that** is strength. **That** is courage. That is what being strong and brave is all about.*

Readings

Another reading might be appropriate at this point. The words to Celine Dion's song 'Fly', beginning 'Fly, fly, little wing / Fly beyond imagining' are very beautiful and may be read out loud.

If the family have requested religious readings, the 23rd Psalm may also be appropriate.

The following tender readings may also provide comfort to the bereaved.

Goodbye Little One

My little one, you filled my world, heaven sent to me
A sunbeam in a darkened room, a gift from God to see
Your smile, so sweet and tender
You touched my very soul
You helped me grow, strong and tall
That was your little role
You had to go, your time was right, cold emptiness you leave
A life so short, so pure, so loved, hearts you touched—now grieve.

Is it some greater puzzle—I can never understand
I was a mother, parent for a while—I felt so grand
Now all that's left are memories
Framed in black and white
And this pain, deep and tearing
When you flew away from sight
But my little one, my pretty one, when I see the stars above
You will always shine the brightest in the heaven of our love.

Ruth Van Gramberg

A tiny angel face, two sparkling little eyes,
The cutest button nose, our precious sweet surprise.

Mummy loved you dearly, you set Daddy's heart awhirl,
The joy of all the family, our most darling little girl.

You closed your eyes so quickly, you didn't stay for long,
Taken oh so tragically, sweet baby, it seems so wrong.

Divided as we are, we will never be apart,
As you will always live inside your parents' hearts.

Author unknown

When God calls little children to dwell with him above,
We mortals sometimes question the wisdom of His love.

Perhaps God tires of calling the aged to his fold,
So he picks a rosebud before it can grow old.

God knows we need them, and so he takes but few
To make the land of Heaven more beautiful to view.

Believing this is difficult still somehow we must try,
The saddest word we know will always be 'Goodbye'.

So when a little child departs we who are left behind
Must realise God loves children, but angels are hard to find.

Author unknown

Prayers

Again, prayers are appropriate if the bereaved are comfortable with religious elements in the service. You could also take an extract from the Edgar A. Guest poem mentioned earlier, 'To All Parents', particularly the last stanza. Here is another prayer that may be suitable.

Creator and designer of the universe and nature, we commend baby Zoe to you. You care for little children in this present life and for them in the life to come, in a home where they behold your face.

We ask only that Zoe finds another place in your creation where great happiness will be hers. For you have said, 'Let the children come unto me, for the Kingdom of Heaven belongs to such as these'.

May our love for Zoe stay all the more with us because you have taken her. Give us the strength to love each other more and all creation better because of Zoe.

Amen.

Symbolic moments

If there is a symbolic moment to be included in the service, just prior to the committal is an appropriate time to include it. For example, in one infant funeral I conducted at the graveside, each mourner was given three helium balloons of different colours—each one representing the baby's heart, chuckle and tears. On a given word, I asked mourners to let them go and watch the balloons float into the heavens.

You may request that the mourners all hold hands as they say farewell to the lost infant, letting the baby's spirit and strength, and the mourners' love and sorrow, flow through the gathering. You can gently discuss these symbolic parts of the service with the family at the initial interview.

Committal

And now, family and friends, it is time to say our farewell to baby Zoe.

We will always remember baby Zoe. We will live our daily lives more fully, with integrity of purpose, cheerfulness and love.

From the midst of our mourning we leave this service knowing love is never changed, or lost, by death.

Tenderly and reverently we commit the body of precious Zoe to the universe, from which all life comes and to which all life, in the end, returns.

We are glad Zoe lived. We are glad we saw her lovely face, so much like her mother and father.

We are glad we held her tiny hand and felt her touch. We cherish the memory of the joy and beauty she brought to us.

In token of our love for Zoe, we will resolve to offer a generous affection to each other so far as we are able, and to the young children of humanity the world over. We leave Zoe in peace and bid her farewell.

There are no words of comfort adequate to overcome the sadness the family will feel as a diminutive casket holding an infant's tiny body is lowered into a tiny grave.

Service for a stillborn baby

Imagine an expectant mother joyously going to hospital to give birth and to bring home a precious baby. Imagine the grief, the pain, the numbing sense of loss when the baby arrives, and is still, having never taken his first breath. In this situation, the parents will be utterly, intensely devastated. They will feel lost, helpless, unutterably grief-stricken.

As the celebrant, this is one of the most heart-wrenching circumstances you will face. You will need to sit with the parents as they express their sorrow and, through the tears and the expectations of what might have been, gain sufficient knowledge to write a service. The parents may wish to show you the nursery, the baby clothes, the things they have bought in readiness for their baby's arrival.

Even though a stillborn baby has not had a chance to live, many parents will want to name their baby. When I have been in this situation, I have suggested the parents do choose a name that I will use during the service.

This type of service will be a unique challenge. Your opening remarks might be along these lines:

> *We come here this morning to this beautiful, peaceful place to commit the body of baby Ethan, the precious little boy of Leanne and Tim, to the earth.*
>
> *He was a tiny little ray of sunshine that danced and shone inside our hearts. A little life has been taken before it even began.*
>
> *Baby Ethan did not have the opportunity to breathe, to laugh or to cry. He was, however, lovingly nurtured through those months as he grew, wriggled and kicked, making Leanne and Tim aware that he was waiting to become their beloved child.*
>
> *We grieve today for the life that did not happen and for the life that Leanne and Tim did not have with Ethan.*

Then you might continue the service with readings, tributes and prayers as described earlier in the chapter.

10 Servicemen and women, and Rotarians

At this particular time, the many great men and women who served so bravely in the terrible wars are all reaching an age when their mortality is beginning to touch them. Many are proud members of service organisations like the Returned and Services League of Australia (RSL). The war service of these people may be seen by their families as a key characteristic that should be given a central place in the funeral service.

Other members of the community may belong to organisations such as Rotary and the Freemasons, and these too can bring some particular elements and rituals into funeral services. In my experience, preparing a service for members of these groups is a special challenge worthy of a chapter of its own. In this section we're going to look at some extracts from sample services that might fit these occasions.

RSL service

Often the family of a deceased serviceman or woman will look into providing an RSL funeral service. Sometimes, however, members from the RSL are unfortunately not available to bestow that honour on their comrade. This may happen in rural areas where distance, and the lack of a local RSL sub-branch, make an RSL presence impossible.

When this happens, a celebrant can step in and fill the void. The service will lack the presence of qualified ex-servicemen and women, and the atmosphere of official remembrance that they bring to the occasion, but as a celebrant you can do your best to bring this feeling to the service.

Opening words

If the service is conducted by a member of the RSL, announce:

> *In honour of their comrade, [name of RSL member] of the [name of sub-branch] Sub-Branch of the RSL will now conduct an RSL service.*

If it is not to be conducted by an RSL member, I commence the service by telling a true story.

As a lead-in to a special RSL service for Bert, I would like to tell you a true story. It is a story almost too sacred to be told.

In Kohima, in Borneo, there stands a huge monolith, commemorating the servicemen who lost their lives in World War II.

In a vast cemetery there are rows and rows of crosses depicting the New Zealand, American and Australian servicemen who gave up their lives. On the walls of the monolith are listed the names of the servicemen, and across the arch of the monolith is carved an inscription in large letters which reads:

When you go home
Tell them of us and say
For your tomorrow
We gave our today.

I believe they are the most eloquent words that came out of those terrible years. So simple, so true, so meaningful, yet so challenging.

Today you and I have all the luxuries of life that one can imagine—we go to the well of life, taking its wealth and its pleasures, and we take from it life's treasures, but forgotten are those who dug the well. We should never forget who dug that well.

Bert Anderson was one of those who dug the well.

Some words about the deceased

We know that Bert served his country well in World War II, throughout the Pacific. He was one those who gave us our nation and our future.

The depth of commitment required to serve his country at time of war will only really be known by those who served with and alongside him. We who remain, who never served, can only marvel at the generosity of spirit it takes to offer your life for your country. Their bodies lie in peace and their names live for forever.

O valiant hearts to whom your glory came,
Through dust of conflict and through battle flame;
Tranquil you lie, your knightly virtue proved,
Your memory hallowed in the land you loved.

Proudly you gathered, rank on rank, to war
As who had heard God's message from afar;
All you had hoped for, all you had, you gave,
To save mankind—yourselves you scorned to save.

Splendid you passed, the great surrender made,
Into the light that never more shall fade.
Deep your contentment in that blest abode,
Who wait the last clear trumpet call of God.

From 'O Valiant Hearts' (hymn), words by John S. Arkwright

You can then invite family members and other returned servicemen and women to place a poppy in an urn, and say:

The hour has come to rest. This poppy—an emblem of sacrifice, the symbol of life offered in the service of one's country—is a link between those who have fallen and those who remain. We place it in remembrance.

Then invite other mourners to come forward and place their poppy in the urn.

I now ask you to preserve a minute's silence in memory of this fallen serviceman, Bert Harold Anderson.

Music

At this point, 'The Last Post' and 'Reveille' are played.

Closing

Ask all to stand, then recite 'The Ode':

> *They shall grow not old as we that are left grow old.*
> *Age shall not weary them nor the years condemn.*
> *At the going down of the sun, and in the morning,*
> *We will remember them.*

> *[All say] Lest we forget.*

You may then like to finish with the following prayer, carried by Eleanor Roosevelt as she visited troops in war zones during World War I:

> *Dear Lord,*

> *Lest I continue my complacent way, help me to remember that somewhere, somehow out there, a man died for me today.*

> *As long as there be war, I then must ask and answer, 'Am I worth dying for?'*

Tribute for a serviceman or woman

Here is one way you may incorporate a tribute into a service for an ex-serviceman or woman.

> *We meet to pay tribute to one who served with us in the defence forces of the nation. Colin's ex-service friends will know how well he served, while many will have shared his community responsibility through his longtime involvement in the National Servicemen's Association of Australia.*

Here you might recount some personal details of the deceased's war service and life.

> *Remembering these qualities, now lost to us, we recognise the need to maintain the national service tradition of continuing unselfish service, involving the care of others, particularly those with disabilities, the bereaved, or those in need.*

At this point you can hold up a flower, and invite others to place a flower on the coffin.

As a token of affection and proud remembrance, I place here this flower and I invite all ex-servicemen and women to join in so doing.

Now I ask you to join me, reverently, in a silent tribute to our beloved comrade Colin Stanley Wilson.

'The Last Post' and 'Reveille' are then played, and 'The Ode' recited, as for the RSL service above.

Service for a Legatee

The families of Legatees—that is, members of Legacy—may choose to include the following during a funeral service, or at its end.

First, the president or deputy of the local Legacy club is invited to come forward to conduct the service. The president then invites other members of Legacy to come forward and form a semi-circle around the coffin or the grave.

The president or deputy will then deliver an address.

A laurel wreath is then placed on the coffin by the speaker (or, if at the graveside, the speaker lets the wreath fall on the coffin), and the following reading is delivered:

Fear not that you have served for nought,
the torch you threw to us we caught!

And now our hands will hold it high,
its glorious light shall never die!

We'll not break faith with you who lie
on many a field.

The Legacy speaker then leads a prayer.

Let us pray.

In silence with thankful hearts let us remember the life and work of our comrade, together with all those, especially his comrades, who made the supreme sacrifice.

Legatees—our departed comrade.

*O thou who crowned the mystery of life with thine unchanging
love, we commend to thy loving care all those who are suffering or
bereft. Grant to each of us to whom this legacy has been committed
a sense of great privilege—a keen desire to hold aloft the torch of
remembrance and an enthusiasm to serve—so that when we too shall
answer the last summons we may be found faithful even unto death.*

Amen.

The speaker then asks the mourners to observe a minute's silence. At its conclusion, the speaker says 'Lest we forget', and Legatees respond with the same words.

To finish, 'The Last Post' is played, or the General Salute if it is a military funeral.

Service for a Rotarian

If you are called upon to conduct a service for a Rotarian, then the following prayer is acceptable to all Rotarians.

Let us pray.

*Eternal spirit, from whom we come, to whom we belong, and in whose
presence is our peace and joy, grant us now such spiritual triumph in
the memory of our fellow Rotarian in whose character and service
we rejoice.*

*We thank you for the Club and the opportunities it gave him to fulfil
his desires to serve the common good.*

*We are grateful for the friends we have made, the fellowship we
enjoy, the accomplishments for the happiness of others; and we
acknowledge the sincere and active part Charles has played in the
enjoyment of those benefits.*

*In Rotary's ideal of service 'Service Above Self', we commit ourselves
anew to:*

Truth in word and deed
Fairness to all concerned
Goodwill and better friendships
Beneficence to all concerned

And pray for humility in your power, strength in our weakness, dignity in service, guidance in our movements, and your blessing in our plannings.

For your love's sake,

Amen

Reverend David Ryrie and Reverend Geoff Browne

11 *Special services*

Sometimes, as a funeral celebrant, you will be asked to perform a special kind of service. In this chapter we will look at a Christmas memorial service, a tree-planting memorial and a service for the internment of ashes.

Christmas memorial service

At Christmas I have had the honour of being part of a service dedicated to those who have passed in the preceding 12 months. The service is held in December, and arranged by a funeral director who invites the families and friends of departed loved ones.

During the service those in attendance are invited to come forward and, in remembrance of their loved one, place a card with their private message on a special memorial tree. The memorial card represents the bearer's grief and pain, and reminds all of the depth of their love for their lost loved one. It represents courage—to confront sorrow, to comfort one another, and to change lives. It is a way of remembering the times the mourners shared laughter, tears, fun, caring and joy with their lost ones. The memorial tree is therefore a source of hope, reminding all those in attendance of the love and sacred memories they will have forever.

The program for the service comprises appropriate musical items, prayers and speeches by both a religious and a civil celebrant. The poignant finale is the placing of memorial cards on the tree, after which afternoon tea is served.

Celebrant's speech

When asked to speak to you today, I was very reluctant. What feelings can I express to you that you have not already experienced? But to say no would be remiss of me, for surely I have learned something from the funerals I have conducted and the association I have been privileged to have with the loved ones of those lost to us.

My first encounter with those suffering from the loss of a loved one is always the hardest. There I am met with a great range of emotions—anger, despair, pain, sorrow, blame, confusion, loneliness, depression, bitterness and sometimes even relief when there has been a sickness. My role is to comfort, and with their help compose a meaningful, comforting and realistic service.

From the passing of the elderly, which is more a celebration of a life that has encompassed achievement and fulfilment, to those in the prime of life with mountains to climb, rivers to cross and challenges to meet, to the trauma of accidents, to the pressures of life confronting young people, even to a recent four-month-old baby, I never cease to admire the fortitude of people, and the strength and unity of friendship and love.

When we lose a loved one, time seems to stand still. We are faced with the past, the present and the future all at once. The past, when everything was okay, is too painful to contemplate. The present, in which we are seized with grief, dominates everything. It seems endless, all-pervading, crushing. And as for the future, whatever it was to hold has been totally wiped out. It becomes a jumble of shattered dreams, utterly destroyed.

Time and again, I hear people say, 'I'll never get over it' or 'I'll never forget it'—and nor should we, because we should cherish the memory of that person. But it is essential that we become comfortable with that, for we are not meant to go on locked in suffering, unable to move on.

Here is a story. A famous tenor was giving a recital at Carnegie Hall when his wife, sitting in the audience, became ill. She was rushed to hospital, where later she died. Overcome with grief, the singer vowed he would never sing again. True to his vow, his golden voice from that day remained silent.

Three years after the loss of his wife, on Christmas Eve, he visited his sister, who was ill, in hospital. She persuaded him to accompany her to the hospital auditorium where a soprano was to give a recital and lead the patients and staff in Christmas carols. The minutes ticked by, and an announcement was made that the soprano had double-booked and there would be no concert or carols that evening.

Suddenly the famous tenor rose from his seat, walked down the aisle, climbed the stairs to centre stage and began to sing 'The Holy City'. For two hours he sang beautiful popular arias and led the audience in Christmas carols. Once again the magnificent voice of the tenor was heard.

I tell that story only to emphasise that we must not let grief dictate our lives. It is so important that we face the future with courage, acceptance and optimism, for this is our healing time. We must adjust to our loss and learn to continue our lives without that person. Now all of this is no small task, no small responsibility—it takes courage and moral strength to let go and move on.

There are some words that say:

Miss me a little but not with your head bowed low.
Remember the joy and love that once we shared.
Memory is the treasury and keeper of all things.
Miss me—but let me go.

And how do we do this? How do we heal?

I get quite cross when I hear someone offering the advice, however well-meant, that 'time heals all wounds'. Because it is not the passage of time itself that brings resolution, but the way we work through the stages of grief.

First, it is essential to realise just what grief is. Grief is love, and it is because we feel such pain—because the inner ache is so great—that we know the depth of our love. Grief simply cannot and does not exist except where there has been love.

Grief is not a mountain to be climbed, with the strong reaching the summit long before the weak. Grief is not an athletic event with stopwatches timing our progress. Grief is a walk through loss and pain. There is no competition and no time trials.

I believe it is essential that we make our lost loved ones part of our future lives. A way we can do this is to accept the fact that they have left us, but give them a continuing stake in how we live. In this way, they are not just part of the past in our memories or of the present, but will continue to live and to achieve through whatever we have taken from their lives and added to our own for the benefit of others. And by doing this, we can feel a wonderful closeness to them, even listening for their voice.

But don't be afraid to grieve, for grief is an expression of your love. Think about, talk about and treasure your memories of your loved one, and be your own timekeeper. Heal in your own way and in your own time. The experience of grief is powerful. So, too, is your ability to help yourself to heal. In doing the work of grieving, you are moving toward a renewed sense of meaning and purpose in your life.

The beautiful serenity prayer says:

God grant us the serenity to accept the things we cannot change, the courage to change the things we can, and the wisdom to know the difference.

And those simple words mean change what you can, but accept what you cannot.

Here is another story. The place: a barn in Russia. The day: Christmas Eve, 1900. The event: a Christmas worship attended by peasants. The sleet pounded the roof of the barn like a giant whip. Halfway through the service, the door to the barn was thrust open. An officer entered, followed by members of the secret police.

The officer lined up the peasants against the barn wall and counted them: 'One, two, three … thirty-one, thirty-two.'

Suddenly a voice with a ring of steel said, 'You have missed one!'

Again the officer counted, 'One, two, three … thirty-one, thirty-two. See, you silly old fool, there are thirty-two!' shouted the officer.

'No,' said the voice of steel again. 'You have missed one. For wherever there are two or more gathered in my name, there will I be.'

Why did I tell you that story? Well, there is a family I have kept in touch with who never commence their Christmas dinner without a moment's silence for their lost loved one. 'It's as if Dad is with us,' says the daughter, 'and after that moment's silence the family just grows in stature, togetherness, fun and fellowship.'

In Albury, there a group of dedicated people called The Palliative Care. I call them 'God's Angels'. A very prominent elderly lady passed away and the family were having great difficulty in coming to terms with their loss. I was a little apprehensive about the quality of my service when five minutes before it was due to begin Sister Kate, the Sister in charge of The Palliative Care, slipped me a piece of paper containing the following words.

The paper contained the poem 'Imagine' by Yvonne Goddard, and I read out the words of this moving tribute. The full text of the poem is in Chapter 5.

Now while those words are comforting, some might say they are fantasy. But now let me read one of my favourite verses from the scriptures and to me the meaning is the same. John chapter 14, verses 1–6, says:

Jesus promised his followers a place in his Father's house.

He said to them, 'Let not your heart be troubled; believe in God, believe also in me. In my Father's house are many rooms; if it were not so, would I have told you that I go to prepare a place for you? And when I go and prepare a place for you, I will come again and take you to myself, that where I am you may be also. And you know the way where I am going.'

Thomas said to him, 'Lord, we do not know where you are going; how can we know the way?'

Jesus said to him, 'I am the way, and the truth, and the life; no one comes to the Father, but by me.'

Well, now, I'd better give you a laugh. It was time during the church service for the children's sermon. The minister invited all the children to come forward. One little girl was wearing a beautiful dress. The minister leant over and said, 'That is a very pretty dress.' The little girl replied directly into his microphone, 'Yes, but my mum says it is a real bitch to iron.'

I guess that's enough from me, but if my words have had any meaning at all, then let it be this: in accepting the reality of loss, a change will occur in our values and priorities. Things that once seemed important may become unimportant and things that were unimportant may take on a new significance. When our values and priorities change, so do our lives.

Let us strive together, and succeed in overcoming the grief that comes from our love. Let us recognise the beauty and the purpose of these lost lives, and make those lives part of our own lives. Let them add to our growth, and the quality and strength of our character.

Placing the memorial cards

Here are some words for our departed loved ones.

Our memorial cards represent our grief. They are also the light of our love for you. As we enter the holiday season, day by day we cherish the special place in our hearts that will always be reserved for you. We thank you for the gift of your life as we place our memorial cards on the tree in honour of you. We place them for our grief, our courage, our memories, our love and our hope.

Each person will have written the name of their lost loved on a memorial card. They are then asked to come forward and place their card on a branch of the tree.

Our memorial cards are in our memories. They are the times we laughed together, the times we cried, the times we were angry with each other, the silly things we did, and the caring and joy we gave each other.

And our memorial tree is the source of hope, for it reminds us of love, and memories of you that are ours forever.

We love you.

Tree-planting memorial

I once conducted a memorial ceremony for a relatively young man—we will call him Jason—who tragically met his death in a factory accident. Twelve months later, on the anniversary of his passing, I was asked to conduct a tree-planting ceremony at the factory where he had died.

Family, close friends, management and staff gathered around the young tree.

Thank you for inviting me to share this time of remembrance for Jason. I commend you all for this honour that you have bestowed upon him.

It is very easy to go along with the old time-honoured sayings—'Time heals all wounds', or 'Out of sight, out of mind'. But today we are once again honouring a lost workmate.

We remember his fine qualities of character—honesty, sincerity, thoughtfulness, caring and fair-play. We honour him as a dedicated employee, a hard worker, a wonderful son, a loving brother, a fun-loving uncle and friend.

I talked about Jason's particular qualities and the details of his life, and then continued:

For a tree to reach maturity it must be deep-rooted—like Jason, who as a young boy was brought up by a family who held sacred the time-honoured qualities of honesty, integrity, example and goodwill to others.

For a tree to grow tall it has to grow straight—as Jason did, growing in wisdom, understanding and concern for his fellow man.

For a tree to grow strong it has to be fed—like Jason, growing in character by giving of his heart, mind and capacity in all his endeavours.

A tree must face bravely the vagaries of nature, wind, storms, frost and heat—like Jason, facing life with its ups and downs.

A tree, when mature, offers shade and comfort to those in need—like Jason did in the giving of himself, friendship, help, support, love and warmth to others.

A tree welcomes the dawn—as Jason did, making each day better than yesterday, tomorrow better than today.

A tree bows before the sunset—as Jason closed each day knowing he had given his best.

I therefore, on behalf of you, the management of [factory name], you his workmates, and you his loving family and friends, honour the memory of Jason, and dedicate this tree in his name, knowing that, like Jason, this tree will grow tall, straight, strong and true.

I then invited a selected group—a representative of the factory's management, a workmate and a family member—to unveil the plaque for Jason. Others were then invited to turn the soil for the tree-planting. The factory shut down for the rest of the day in his honour, and a gathering was held afterwards to pay tribute.

Service for the internment of ashes

Sometimes, a family may request you to conduct a ceremony for the internment of ashes in a cemetery, or in a sacred place chosen by the family or the deceased before their passing.

This may be under a rose tree in a cemetery, scattered over the waters of a lake, river or ocean, or even at the home of a family member or friend. The following is an example of what you might say at such a service.

Earth to earth.

Ashes to ashes.

Dust to dust.

We commit these ashes of our dearly beloved ----. In placing the ashes of ---- in this hallowed ground, we think again of all that our loved companion, [sister, wife, husband, brother, grandfather, grandmother, etc.] and friend has meant to us.

And we dedicate this simple plot, amid these natural surroundings, to every beautiful and precious memory associated with ----.

We lay these ashes in that gentle earth, which has been the chief support of humans since first we walked beneath the sun, from which all life comes and to which all life in the end returns.

To all human beings, to all living forms, the soil has ever provided the sustenance that is the staff of life.

To that good earth we now commit the ashes of ---- and we are grateful for the life that has been lived; and for all that life has meant to us.

We are glad ---- lived. We are glad we saw her face and felt the pressure of her hand. We cherish the memories of her words, her deeds and her character. We cherish her friendship.

But most of all we cherish her love.

Ashes to ashes, dust to dust,
Memory to memory, story to story.

Blessing to blessing, strength to strength,
Gratitude to gratitude, spirit to spirit.

Love to love, the wheel turns ever,
And what came out of the earth,
Returns to it now in peace.

Benediction

May you find strength and support in your love for one another and may you find peace in your hearts.

Let us now leave this sacred place in quietness of spirit and live with care, love and concern for one another.

PART
4

Some Inspiration

12 *Inspirational words and phrases*

If your aim is to improve the descriptive words and phrases in your service, this final chapter is one you may find very useful. Whether you are a brilliant orator, an average speaker, or one who lacks confidence, the following inspirational words and phrases can be a great resource that will help you become a more fluent funeral celebrant.

At any funeral service, the emphasis should not be on *how* you present but the words you say, particularly in the eulogy. Not everyone will be a naturally brilliant speaker or public presenter, but sincerity, clarity, preparation and some practice in the careful choice of words, you will be able to convey the important meaning behind what you say. This forms the basis for a very memorable service.

The words and phrases in this chapter will help you to adequately describe a person—their personality, their achievements and the life they have lived—in the personal, business, social, community, sporting and academic realms. If you strive to be sincere and to represent the deceased as remembered by family and friends, you will have fulfilled your duty as a celebrant.

While speaking plainly and from the heart is the most important thing, using imagery and thoughtful phrasing will bring comfort to mourners who wish to celebrate the life of their loved one. For example:

- Rather than simply saying, 'She was a successful woman', try something like, 'Her family and friends are mourning the loss of a mentor, a leader and a champion.'

- Instead of 'He did wonderful community service work', you might say, 'He gave of his mind, his heart and his full capacity in the service of others.'

Examine, nurture, mould and use the following words of inspiration to create a eulogy that the family and mourners will appreciate and remember.

Phrases for people and personalities

Adventurousness

She was never one to let the grass grow under her feet.

His life reads like an adventure story.

Her special quality was an adventurous spirit. Whatever the event, whatever the challenge, she was there in full force.

He touched the youthful thirst for heroics.

She swept all along in her wake, setting a dizzying pace as she sought to devour every sight and sound possible.

He dared to be different.

She had an infectious zest for living which remained with her until the very end.

Ambition and achievement

Anything he set his sights on received every ounce of his considerable mind, body and spirit that he could muster. If his life was a cricket match, he gave it the full face of the bat—he quite simply did not know any other way.

If she decided she wanted to do something, she would achieve it.

He had high expectations of himself and of those around him.

She demanded of others what she sought in herself—excellence in all things.

He wholeheartedly believed that the secret of success was to never give up.

She had a great belief in the future and an ability to forget the past. She lived in the future, always marvelling at the great potential it held.

He was a winner who gave his all.

She was an extraordinary, rare person whose touch could turn everything to gold.

He will be remembered for his legendary achievements.

(See also *Professional success*.)

Charm and charisma

He was a colourful character—a raconteur.

She always had a story for you, delivered with a smile and an impish wink of the eye.

He was a good-natured, fun-loving larrikin with a warm heart and caring nature. That laidback approach to life his friends and family loved belied a sharp intellect—his cleverness was something he never advertised, never promoted.

She was a wonderful woman—a diamond in the rough who left a mark on everyone she met.

Courage

She was very vigorous, very forthright and never once shrunk from the effort life demanded of her.

He was passionately proud of his heritage and fought for it on the battlefield.

She never flinched, never ducked for cover, and was always consistent in her manner and life.

His weathered exterior was the face of a great deal of substance, courage and warmth.

She was one of the wisest, the bravest and the best.

His extraordinary courage in facing his approaching death was remarkable.

Her courage inspired those around her and endeared her to those who cared for her.

To some, these would seem like handicaps, but for ---- they became his greatest gifts, and he shared them with everyone through the whole of his life.

Creative thinking

She had a kaleidoscope of talents, ideas and thoughts that would seize you in their breathtaking liveliness and passion.

He was a visionary, an animator, who breathed life into projects and ideas.

She was immersed in the creativity that was generated through bringing people together.

He had a vision of life that I can only describe as panoramic.

She was creative, talented and had the ability to turn something ordinary into something extraordinary.

He was never afraid to think outside the square and do something.

Her creative talents knew no bounds, and everything she accomplished was infused with her artistic flair.

He was an entrepreneur and a lateral thinker.

Family and parenthood

She was a tireless mother whose last words spoke of her love and concern for her family.

He was a loving, generous and proud father.

She was inspirational in her devotion and care for her family.

He was, first and foremost, a loving husband and father of impeccable strength.

She breathed life, love and heart into all her family activities.

In all of the hectic schedule of his life, his time for his family was of paramount importance and his love and mateship helped all to grow.

To the world she was but one woman, but to her family she was the world.

He was an example to his family, instilling in his children the importance of helping others. He placed the highest value on family.

She passionately maintained family traditions and loved to stay abreast of the achievements of every family member.

When he was not working he would spend time escaping with his family, which made for a rich childhood for his three children.

She always trumpeted the achievements of her family, whether they were large or small.

He described his grandchildren as the highlight of his life and never missed an opportunity to spoil them.

But above all else, she was a wife, mother, grandmother, great-grandmother and friend, and will be remembered for the energy and dedication she brought to these roles.

Above all else, he can be remembered as a loving, generous and caring granddad, and the sense of importance that he gave that role.

Her fierce and undying commitment to her family stayed with her to the very end.

Generosity and selflessness

His generous spirit will never be forgotten.

She was always aware of the people around her—their interests, their hopes, their dreams and their inspirations. What better way to remember her than to serve our friends as ---- served hers?

He was always willing to help others and could be relied upon to brighten the day of those around him.

She lived for those she loved.

He had the ability to give and to grace the lives of others with unconditional love.

She befriended those in need and sought to assist the less fortunate wherever possible.

He was a man whose professionalism, friendship and willingness to help has left an indelible mark on those he has touched and helped throughout his life.

She was a great listener who put herself in others' shoes.

She left a legacy of care, kindness, commitment and involvement in the heart of her family and community.

He was a man who loved his fellow man, and who unselfishly and consistently demonstrated it with his kind, generous and thoughtful deeds.

He was an extraordinary contributor to the community.

She did volunteer work because she loved it. She didn't add up the hours each week — it was the quality of work she did that counted.

He gave of his heart, mind and spirit.

She was forever thinking of others. There was never a favour passed up or a request turned down.

He was always loving and giving, no matter what — always putting others before himself.

She touched so many people, so many lives, in a positive way because of her giving nature.

He lived for what he could do for people.

She touched so many people — so many lives — in a positive way because of her giving nature.

Always reaching out to others, he enriched so many lives through his tireless efforts.

Throughout life she touched people with a generosity of spirit, encouraging them to seek out new challenges.

He made you believe in yourself and see that you could succeed in whatever you chose to do.

Her great strength was that she unfailingly placed the needs of others above her own.

Through his love for humanity he made a positive difference to the lives of many who came into contact with him.

She was a selfless and active person, with a mighty social conscience and an unflinching desire to care for others less fortunate than herself.

He believed that the path to happiness was by giving.

(See also *Love and kindness*.)

Happiness and cheerfulness

One of his strongest characteristics was his happiness, his laugh and the light of sheer joy in his eyes. These are the things those who knew him well will recall when they think of him.

She was renowned for her infectious smile.

The broad grin and twinkle in his eyes will provide enduring memories for those who

loved him.

She had a ready smile and happy personality.

He passionately believed that your day was as good as you made it.

She was blessed with a long and happy life.

(See also *Sense of humour*.)

Hard work and tirelessness

She was a person who had an enormous capacity for work and getting things done.

He understood the reality of working life but was also visionary—and more than a little romantic about he believed society could be.

She was someone you could always turn to if you needed to get the job done.

He added value to everything he did—his work, the community, his family.

She was not afraid to get her hands dirty.

Humility and gentleness

She didn't make a fuss about things—she just got on with what needed to be done.

He had the right to be but was never conceited, vain, big-headed, puffed up or smug. Never did he become his own hero.

She was a modest, shy and diffident person. She did not push herself forward; rather she was a facilitator and a connector.

He was extremely unassuming yet mightily effective.

She was a person of simple tastes and gentle ways.

He was a quiet, no-fuss achiever.

She rarely spoke of her heroic feats.

He has left behind a great legacy in the community by living a simple and honourable life.

She was a truly a gentle and caring person who had time for everyone. When you were in her company, you felt special.

He was blessed with a gentle nature and simple outlook on life.

Imperfections

He was a remarkable man in many ways. He had a gruff manner but was, at heart, a bit of a softie. He could be cantankerous and difficult, but if you needed help, he'd be the first right there beside you.

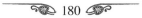

She was a great believer that the mistakes in one's life were opportunities to learn something new.

His common failings made him real.

Integrity

He was a man of principle and compassion, and he was loved, admired and respected by those he came into contact with.

She had an innate sense of decency and integrity.

He never faltered in being true to himself and the standards he set.

She was a woman who demonstrated total commitment to her beliefs, who led by example and who commanded enduring respect from all who were fortunate enough to have known her.

He was a man of integrity who treated all people equally—with respect, dignity and fairness.

She stood firmly by her principles, morals and ethical beliefs to the last, and possessed a fundamental decency that shone like a beacon through the good times and the bad.

He was kind, fair and wise in all his undertakings.

She never judged anyone else for their actions, and people felt free to express their opinions in her home.

With a deep common sense and an innate decency and integrity, ---- was nobody's lieutenant but a prince among men.

Intelligence

When he spoke, it was with all the subtle elegance contained in the English language.

She will be remembered as an immensely gifted person who could speak to anyone, at any level, with subtlety and intelligence.

People from all walks of life and cultural backgrounds sought his counsel.

Choices determine one's life. She made the right choices.

He established a giant reputation not only for his undisputed knowledge of the law in all its facets, but for his integrity and humanity.

Her restless intellect and inquiring mind will be missed.

He was a very astute judge of people.

Her intellectual energy, her hospitality and the joy she found in her work will continue to resonate through our lives.

He had an analytical and mathematical mind. His budgeting and sports statistics filled reams of paper, with everything meticulously recorded and analysed.

She wanted to explore her capabilities, her potential and her intelligence, and actively challenged herself to expand her mind.

His deliberations and opinions earned him respect and admiration.

Leadership

He was a born leader—a colossus of a man, an institution, a person of great intellect and impeccable character, who combined candour with simplicity, integrity and dignity.

She was a tireless, loyal and inspirational leader, and a wise and willing confidant.

He presented a tall, handsome and imposing figure and his carefully chosen words, delivered in a well-modulated voice, never failed to gain the support of his listeners.

She became a trusted confidant, a loyal friend and a wise mentor to those who crossed her path.

He has had an influence and made a difference.

She was a teacher and a guide to others, and believed that everyone had potential—it just had to be discovered.

He was a champion in an exciting and revolutionary period.

(See also *Professional success*.)

Love and kindness

Her life was a lesson in loyalty, kindness and steadfastness.

His caring and compassionate qualities became even more selfless with his devotion to his beloved [name of partner].

She was a beautiful woman who believed that love was the essence of everything beautiful and the force behind everything wonderful.

He believed that everything done with love would last.

She truly believed in the circle of care—that you couldn't receive love and kindness without giving them back in full measure.

The giving of self through love is the greatest pleasure life can give—and we will remember ---- as someone who lived by that.

She believed her life was defined by the people she loved.

He knew more than anyone that love makes good people.

She was a shining example of the words of Mother Teresa:

'Love not in words but love until it hurts.'

(See also *Generosity and selflessness*.)

Optimism

She lived always with high optimism—to make every year better than her last.

He had an adventurous spirit and always looked on the bright side, hoping to make today better than yesterday, and tomorrow better than today.

She did not dwell on what could have been, but appreciated all she had.

He firmly believed that there was a light at the end of every tunnel and that the sun returned after every storm.

She was someone who was forever turning negatives into positives.

He had a commitment to life—to his plans, his hopes and his dreams.

Passion and enthusiasm

His personal life was lived with the same passion as his professional life. He was an incessant writer of letters to the editor, repository of the family history, cook and devotee of good mystery novels.

She was dedicated to the things she loved in her life.

His skills and hobbies were enough for ten men.

Everything she did was done with passion, zeal and enthusiasm.

Professional success

She was an honest, hardworking and successful [name of job].

He was the driving force behind [name of company].

Her code was simply to do the best she could. The result was excellence.

He was an intelligent, energetic, determined and committed man, as is borne out by the range and extent of his achievements.

The people in the industry are mourning the loss of a mentor, a leader and a champion.

Many of his successes in life can be attributed to his attitude.

She took pride in her position and every day did the best job she could.

His methodology was brilliant and uncomplicated and he plied a devastating trade.

She made a tangible difference in the [name of industry] world. She was known for her passion, dedication and focus. She had the ability to see any problem clearly and to define it with a simplicity that made creative solutions possible.

He immediately impressed the community with his energy, vision and clear-sighted understanding of the demands of the position. He was gentle in his dealings with his colleagues and with the wider community.

She was a person who polarised opinions—and that is a major reason for her success.

His achievements and work ethic were governed by the principles of honesty, total effort, and the giving of heart, mind and spirit. These are the guidelines to follow if you want to succeed and be the very best you can.

She found her niche as a successful businesswoman, admired and respected by her clients and colleagues.

His philosophy was that it didn't matter whether you were loved or hated—it was whether you were respected that really mattered.

When she retired it left a huge hole in the [name of industry] industry.

(See also *Leadership*.)

Sense of humour

He was unfailingly good-tempered, with a great sense of humour.

She was a happy-go-lucky person—someone who could see the funny side of every circumstance, and who could laugh at herself in any predicament.

He was a stirrer, a teaser and a practical joker.

She loved a laugh and enjoyed having people on.

He allowed nothing to be sombre. Having expressed himself with vigour, even with passion, when anything touched the depths of his feelings, he was quick to banish the serious look, to laugh away the serious situation, to smother the bitter disappointment.

There was always much laughter around ----'s home. Her quirky sense of humour, quick wit and talent for storytelling entertained all and sundry.

He was a man who could laugh at himself.

(See also *Happiness and cheerfulness*.)

Sense of justice

She always felt obliged to right the wrongs she came across.

He quietly refused to accept injustice, and believed that by working together you could achieve anything.

She had a towering sense of ambition, overshadowed only by a driving need to encourage fair play.

He was a man who would listen to and support anyone who he believed had a right and just cause.

She was passionate about everyone's right to live in a fairer society.

He died doing what he thought was right—and he loved doing it.

Sociability

He threw himself into life and thoroughly enjoyed the company of others, especially in his school days.

She knew that if you wanted to make friends, then you should be a friend, for friendship is a priceless gift.

He was a quiet bloke but when he spoke everyone listened.

She had a turn of phrase to suit most people and situations.

In his own special way, he would have been more than happy at this packed chapel on the day of his funeral.

She was a genuine people person. She had great communication skills and the gift to be able to understand people from all walks of life.

In all of his [no. of years] years he lived every day to the full, simply touching the lives of those he met and befriended.

Sporting prowess

A supreme technician, he did not have to change his game over the passage of time.

She was so good she spawned generations of imitators.

He was imperturbable in the heat of battle.

Off the field, she was also a winner.

He had a heart as big as Phar Lap.

She carved out a impressive swag of records.

He wasn't an overly big bloke but was as hard as nails and super-fit.

Her record underpinned her unstinting excellence against a great range of opponents.

Statistically and athletically, he had no peer.

Winning was never the issue—she said it was the way you played the game. However, she almost never lost.

They said he would not face up to the fact that the competition would be too much for him, but he was a champion and champions rise to any challenge and condition.

She had a vision and a dream to be a champion.

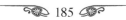

As the world heavyweight boxing champion Jack Dempsey once said: 'A champion is someone who gets up when he can't'.

She had guts, style, honesty an unshakeable belief in herself.

Strength

All her life she was the rock, the solid place, the one to whom her family turned in times of need.

He was made of something that was really solid.

She retained her equilibrium under the most stressful circumstances.

His greatness was not measured in terms of fame or wealth, but in strength of heart and spirit.

She knew how important it was to see through the tough times and to recover from them stronger than ever.

His calm, easygoing and patient nature gave him stability and composure under the greatest of pressures.

Strength during illness

He sought to be a living example of how those with incomplete health still deserved complete human dignity in their remaining years.

Her perseverance and tenacity with an exhausting itinerary despite her age and illness must be explained by her inner faith.

His strength in dealing with his illness was an inspiration to all.

Her inner strength shone through in the way she faced her imminent death.

His last six months were fraught with difficulties but serenity was his hallmark.

Unfortunately she endured sickness for considerable periods during her life, but she never complained and always put her family first.

Wisdom and experience

She gave her experience, knowledge and wisdom to many an emerging career.

He gave himself in service of many causes, where his decisions reflected his wisdom and compassion.

Missed will be her wisdom, her caring, her serenity and her just being there.

He was a man who was a collector of facts and a giver of wisdom, who knew how to apply those facts to the real world.

Her wisdom, thoughtfulness, ability to listen and enthusiasm will remain in the minds of her family and friends.

Other

She was like a snowflake—unique and beautiful in every way.

His combination of personal qualities was extraordinary.

He never forgot his roots and was very proud to have been born and raised in [name of town/region/country].

For the years of friendship, vision and leadership, her spirit will continue to inspire us.

For an ordinary bloke, he was extraordinary.

Her honesty and openness were refreshing; her warmth and wit could melt the hardest of ice.

Nothing was beyond his special attention.

Her remarkable life had many surprising twists.

His great loves were good mates, good beer, red wine, a good steak, a good laugh and good music.

The way she expressed herself, her personal appearance, her home and her way of doing things were unique, original and always stylish.

He had a unique mix of traits—determination, independence and rock-solid morals and values.

She was the most wonderful giver of fun, laughter, warmth and infinite security, and had exquisite taste in so many things.

He was mischievous, generous, adventurous, loyal, considerate, compassionate and a perfectionist.

She was serene and unflappable, courageous and sincere, serious and resolute yet at the same time quick to laugh, and ready with a cheeky, disarming smile.

He will be remembered for his carefree nature, his boisterous love of life, his loyalty and many other qualities that made him a loving husband, fantastic father and steadfast mate.

Most importantly, she did not patronise the young people she served. Her words were straight to the point, challenging them to settle for nothing less than moral perfection.

He was very cheerful, very clever and very kind.

She was an extraordinary spirit on a lifelong search for truth and spiritual enlightenment.

He had a deep love of nature, gardening, films, art and alternative ways of approaching life's challenges.

She was a free thinker and a lover of beautiful things—perfumes, flowers, fabric, clothes, music, art, theatre and nature.

All will miss his friendship, initiative, vibrancy and vitality.

She was known for her down-to-earth personality, dry humour and generosity.

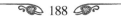

Expressions of loss and comfort

We grieve the loss of somebody who has given so much and had so much more to offer. His loss creates a huge void.

Her life has been distressingly shortened, but we take comfort in the knowledge that in the time that she had, she lived joyfully and made a difference in the world.

He will continue to touch the hearts and minds of people in his death as he did in life.

I believe that there are lessons to be drawn from her life, and from the extraordinary and moving reaction to her passing.

Let's think about him with smiles on our faces and hearts filled with thanks.

Her achievements struck a chord, the depth of which was only apparent in the massive outpouring of grief on her death.

Quotations on life and death

'Our death is not an end if we can live on in our children and the younger generation. For they are us; our bodies are only wilted leaves on the tree of life.'
 —Albert Einstein (1879–1955), German physicist

'Death is not extinguishing the light; it is only putting out the lamp because the dawn has come.'
 —Rabindranath Tagore (1861–1941), Bengali poet and Nobel Prize winner

'I am ready to meet my Maker. Whether my Maker is prepared for the great ordeal of meeting me is another matter.'
 —Winston Churchill (1874–1965), British prime minister

'And in the end, it's not the years in your life that count. It's the life in your years.'
 —Abraham Lincoln (1809–1865), US president

'The fear of death follows from the fear of life. A man who lives fully is prepared to die at any time.'
 —Mark Twain (1835–1910), American writer

'Far better it is to dare mighty things, to win glorious triumphs even though chequered by failure, than to rank with those timid spirits who neither enjoy nor suffer much because they live in the grey twilight that knows neither victory nor defeat.'
 —Theodore Roosevelt (1858–1919), US president and Nobel Peace Prize winner

'The good life is inspired by love and guided by knowledge.'
 —Bertrand Russell (1872–1970), British philosopher, historian and rationalist

Acknowledgments

This book would not have been conceived had certain people not helped me begin my journey into the sacred field of bringing comfort to those who have lost a loved one. My sincere thanks go to Ross Brindley, the proprietor of John Hossack Funeral Services, in Albury, New South Wales.

To Ross Brindley, the perfectionist who taught me the practical aspects of the funeral industry, and how one can experience inspiration and the pursuit of excellence in writing and conducting a funeral ceremony, and comforting others in their personal loss. To Jill Brindley, for her tutorship and mentorship, and to both for their faith in me. And to all those other funeral directors who placed their trust in me.

My grateful thanks to JoJo Publishing for their vision in publishing a book on this subject, and to Emma Driver for editing.

The author and publisher gratefully acknowledge the following persons/ organisations for use of their written material:

Dally R. Messenger, selected text reproduced and adapted with kind permission from the author, from his book Ceremonies & Celebrations: Vows, Tributes and Readings, Lothian, Melbourne, 1999

Ruth Van Gramberg, p.70: 'Cry Not for Me' (extract), p. 114: 'The Shadow of a Man' (adapted), p. 152: 'Goodbye Little One', p.148: 'One So Beloved' reproduced with kind permission of the author, from her book Little Pebbles and Stepping Stones, Australian Federation of Civil Celebrants, Bathurst, 2005.

p.53: Lisa Wroble, 'Within You is the Strength to Meet Life's Challenges'; p.60 & 118: Bessie A. Stanley, 'What constitutes success'; p. 62: Mother Teresa, 'Life is …'; p. 74: James Henry Leigh Hunt, 'Abou Ben Adhem'; p. 84: Grace Noll Crowell, 'Let Me Come In'; p.85 & 113: Yvonne Goddard, 'Imagine'; p. 89: Henry Scott Holland, 'Death is Nothing at All'; p.94: Amelia Josephine Burr, 'A Song of Living'; p. 142: The Compassionate Friends (Victoria) Magazine, 2003; p.157: John S. Arkwright, 'O Valiant Hearts …'; p. 161: Rev. David Ryrie and Rev. Geoff Browne (Rotary Club of Coburg), 'A Prayer for Use at a Rotary Member's Funeral'.

Thank you also to Bob Mahaffey of Albury Legacy Club and Ivon Lofts of the Rotary Club of Coburg for their assistance.

Recommended reading

Barnes, Marian (1992), *Funerals to Celebrate Life: The Positive Value of Creating an Appropriate Funeral*, Simon and Schuster, Sydney.

Messenger, Dally R. (1992), *Ceremonies for Today*, Dally M Publishing and Research, Melbourne.

— — (1999), *Ceremonies & Celebrations: Vows, Tributes and Readings*, Lothian, Melbourne.

York, Sarah (2000), *Remembering Well: Rituals for Celebrating Life and Mourning Death*, Jossey-Bass, San Francisco.

CPSIA information can be obtained
at www.ICGtesting.com
Printed in the USA
LVHW020958050619
620203LV00009B/276/P

9 780987 410320